and I'm going to sleep—but I'm coming out of Vietnam alive, I promise!"

M

Other Avon Books by
John Sack

COMPANY C

JOHN SACK

AVON BOOKS  NEW YORK

About half of this book was first published in *Esquire* in somewhat different form.

AVON BOOKS
A division of
The Hearst Corporation
1350 Avenue of the Americas
New York, New York 10019

Copyright © 1966, 1967, 1968, 1985 by John Sack
Published by arrangement with the author
Library of Congress Catalog Card Number: 84-91654
ISBN: 0-380-69866-8

First Avon Books Printing: March 1985

AVON TRADEMARK REG. U.S. PAT. OFF. AND IN OTHER COUNTRIES, MARCA REGISTRADA, HECHO EN U.S.A.

Printed in the U.S.A.

RA 10 9 8 7 6 5 4 3

1966. In Vietnam, M was assigned to the 1st Infantry Division at Dian and to A, B, and C Companies of the 2d Battalion of the 2d Infantry, in the 3d Brigade of the 1st Infantry Division, at Laikhe. Its first operation was Operation Mastiff, the week of February 21, 1966.

In the Army, a division has about 15,000 men under a major general. Going on down, a brigade has about 4,000 under a colonel, a battalion about 1,000 under a lieutenant colonel or, at training camp, a major, a company about 200 under a captain, a platoon about 40 under a lieutenant, and a squad about 10 under a sergeant.

Lift Your Head and
Hold It High!

dim Olympian entities who reputedly threw cards into an IBM machine or into a hat to determine where each soldier in M would go next, which ones to stay there in the United States, which to live softly in Europe, and which to fight and to die in Vietnam.

No matter. What agonized M this evening wasn't what was in its cards but what was in the more immediate offing—an inspection! indeed, its very first inspection by its jazzy young Negro captain. So this evening M was in its white Army underwear waxing the floor of its barracks, shining its black combat boots, turning the barrels of its rifles inside-out and picking the dust flecks off with tweezers, unscrewing its eardrums—the usual. The air was thick with the smell of floor wax and rifle oil, a moist aroma that now seemed to M to be woven into the very fabric of Army green. Minutes before, the company had heard a do-or-die exhortation from its bantamweight Sergeant Milett. Get yourself clean for *my* sake, Milett had told M. "I've got a wife, three kids at home. I leave in the dark, I come home in the dark. I haven't talked to them thirty-six hours. I don't know, maybe they're dead," using psychology, leaning against a two-decker bed, reaching an arm through the iron bedstead, beseechingly. "Well . . ." making a joke of it, "I left them enough food, I shouldn't have to worry," and getting to the point, "I got a boss downstairs, he got a couple bars on his collar, he is the boss I work for. Tomorrow afternoon he will inspect us: don't make a *jackass* out of me!"

And all you must do is follow the chart! That's all! and M company, now in its fourth quick month of Army life and last of infantry training at a large and bleak Eastern camp, had known what Milett had meant. The strict rectilinear lines of the chart were as clear as those of a chess problem, white to play and to mate in three moves. The chart appeared on the seventy-first page of the *Soldier's Handbook,* the *Handbook* bore the enacting signature of the Army's adjutant general, the general wanted the insides of a guy's green footlocker to be like . . . *so,* and what a proud inspection they'd have if M would just faithfully comply! The scrupulous general had ordered that Pepsodent or any brand of tooth powder that a boy enjoyed must go to the rear of the footlocker, left, it mustn't be dirty or dusty, and it must be bottom backwards so the words TOOTH POWDER appeared upside-down—surprise. The finicky general had charged that a fellow's ꟽAƎᴚƆ ᏄNIʌAHS go to the right while his razor, his blade, his toothbrush, and his comb all covered down on his soap dish; and everything must lie on his whitest towel, the general had commanded. To this Army-wide order of battle a mere master sergeant in M's training camp had dared add an innovation: he allowed that a Bible might lie in between the handkerchiefs and the shoe polish, rightside-up. This would be optional, a matter of conscience; but all other deviations from the archetypical footlocker, the wall locker, the steel combat stuff to be laid on a soldier's bunk, or the soldier himself—would be gigged, Milett had reminded everyone, and gigged would mean no going home Saturday night; no passes.

"So *try.* Follow the chart," he had pleaded and hurried to where his wife and his children, *whew,* still lived, and M, a body of two hundred and fifty Ameri-

.... by exercising his will-o'-the-wisp power. Demirgian built castles in Spain, in Armenia, in any area M wasn't—he dared to have madly escapist flights of imagination because his intuition assured him they'd come to naught. He had said to himself once, *I could walk in front of somebody's rifle.* He had thought he could fall downstairs and tell the doctors, "My brain—it's loose, it's rattling around inside my head," he had come a cropper playing football once and that is how Demirgian's brain had felt, he knew the symptoms. As yet, none of his schemes was a clear and present danger to M's staying at full strength—but Demirgian had a new thought tonight. His fancy had seized on something that a hard-eyed private had said in the course of a 10 o'clock whiskey break, a private who'd been an assistant policeman, a meter maid or something, in his civilian life, who had said to Demirgian that a blow in precisely—*precisely*—the right part of a jaw would break it. Demirgian, his intellect stimulated and his inhibition paralyzed by two J&B's, now replied, "Yaa!" or words to that effect.

"Twenty dollars!" the former policeman cried, whipping a wallet out of his vast Army fatigue pocket, slapping a bill of that denomination on the windowsill, clenching his other fist. "Twenty dollars says I can do it!"

"Yaa! There was a guy twice as big as you, he hit me right *here* and he couldn't break it!"

"That not where I'm going to hit you, Demirgian! Where is your twenty?"

"I'll owe it," already conceding.

"Twenty dollars, Demirgian!" said America's finest, slapping his green gauntlet down for the second time. He had picked up the bill while none of M watched, apparently—he liked its brave sound on the concrete windowsill, *smack!* the sound of Demirgian's jaw cracking like a chicken's wishbone. He didn't like Demirgian anyhow—Demirgian didn't stand tall, as soldiers should. Little small Demirgian slouched, he carried his head tilted like a damn violinist, and when he talked it rolled like a basketball on a rim, nature imitating Brando's art.

"I'll give you an IOU!"

"Shake! Raise up your chin," and Demirgian did. "A little toward the window," and Demirgian did—Demirgian in some dentist chair, his head tilted, jaw slack, his eyes resting precisely on the orange NO SMOKING that was stenciled on M's concrete wall. All of M's sleeping quarters were interior decorated like a city apartment house in its cellar, where the washing machines are. The lengthy low building looked from the outside as though people inside might be working at lathes, and over the black door it announced to all humanity, "M," in black paint.

"Dammit—more to the right."

"I'm waiting. I'm waiting," Demirgian said as in some buried subconscious area he may have thought, *my friends better rescue me*—which seconds later they did.

"Easy . . . easy! Yesterday at the forty-five range he said shoot him in the toes," his tall buddy Sullivan said, stepping between them. "All he wants is get discharged."

"Sure," Demirgian agreed. He had been telling himself, *well . . . either that or I'll make twenty dol-*

lars, the A...

...men's affairs. Already the former policeman was telling guys yes! he had been drinking whiskey but he wasn't drunk, he would straight-line any of them—twenty bucks! but M was back getting ready for that inspection. All of this happened—do understand. Demirgian is real, so is everyone in this account, even the Chillicothe milkman: all about *him* shortly. Names and home towns are in back, middle initials too, apologies to Ernie Pyle.

Anyhow. By 2 in the morning, all of M's fingernails clean, its blankets as tight as a back plaster, its boots luminous, its Brillo-bright combat equipment displayed on its bunks in harmony with the general's chart, at 2 o'clock M company fell asleep in its sleeping bags on the only place left to it—the floor, as infinitesimal iotas of dust silently came to rest on its handiwork, one by one.

M was awakened at 4 o'clock. Today it devolved on the Chaplain to keep it from falling asleep again just after breakfast, for he would be giving M the day's first class. Though his subject, *Courage,* wasn't one notably rich in benzedrine content, the Chaplain, a Protestant major, intended to say things like, "I suggest to you that it takes a man with courage of conviction to—" and here he would strike the flat of his palm against his wooden podium (his pulpit, he called it), jerking M out of its stupor in time to hear him finish his sentence, the text to this surprising gesture—"to put your foot down." He had many tricks, this Chaplain; sometimes he made noises but he had silences, too. He intended to say today, "Do you know what takes courage in a foxhole? It is this," and then he would say, ". . . ," he would say nothing, eons of empty time would go by while everyone's eyes popped open to see if the bottom had dropped out of the universe; and then the Chaplain would say, "It isn't the noises that get you, it's the silence." Also the Chaplain would have some movies.

M got to its vast concrete classroom at 8 o'clock on this piercingly cold winter morning. In the reaches above it, sparrows sat on the heating pipes and made their little squeaking sounds. A sergeant shouted "Seats!" and as M sat down on its cold metal chairs it shouted back in unison, "Blue balls!" or so one might believe until one learned that M had shouted, "Blue bolts!" the nickname of its brigade. M was a shouting company. It built up morale, its high-stepping Negro captain believed; also it kept M awake. Breakfast, lunch, and supper at M were a real bedlam because as each hungry soldier entered the busy messhall he had to left face, stand at attention, and *bellow* at a sergeant the initials signifying whether he had been drafted or had joined the Army voluntarily, *"US, Sergeant!" "RA, Sergeant!"* After meals, the sergeants totaled up each category before reporting it to the mess sergeant, who filed it one whole month before throwing it away.

"Good morning, men," said the Chaplain. He wore his wool winter field clothes with his black scarf, the symbol of the chaplains corps.

"Good morning, sir! Blue bolts! On guard! Mighty mighty Mike! Aargh!" M shouted back. The expression *Blue bolts*—we've been through that. The bri-

... a God-fearing company too. Bibles lay in most of its secular footlockers, a boy from the farm country had a banner with the device TRUST AND OBEY GOD'S WORD as well, folded as trim as a T-shirt in one small unauthorized corner. At night when all M shined itself, eddies of gray light seemed to hang over two or three boys in every platoon room: a Bible in their narrow laps, they sat in white underwear on their steel beds at the other side of the universe from the smell of rifle oil or the *clack, clack,* of bolts being tested, turning the onionskin pages with a jeweler's fingers. This winter morning, one of the quiet listeners to the Chaplain's words was a boy who'd joined the Army because of his having a vision—Smith, the religious soldier's name.

Smith's was a vision with a uniquely American frame. Kneeling in the straw to put rubber milkers on one of his father's holsteins, suddenly in front of Smith's awe-struck eyes the wall of the barn became a giant television screen, and on that apocalyptic channel he had seen a congregation of all this world's white and brown and yellow-skinned peoples, *and many nations shall come, and say, Come, and let us go up to the mountain of the Lord.* And to this ecumenical flock an American man of the cloth was preaching: the minister was Smith himself, an authenticating angel standing behind him, *and he will teach us of his ways, and we will walk in his paths.* But then Smith's dairyman father had come to the barn in dungarees, it was as though he had blown the fuse, the strange vision receded into the walls like so much creosote, there was nothing left but a memory.

"What's the matter?" Smith's father had said.

". . . Nothing."

"You look funny."

". . . I was praying to the Lord."

"Oh that."

But to Smith's receptive mind, the revelation that God had screened on that modest pine siding in Johnstown, New York, was nothing other than the call itself: the Lord wanted him for His minister, so it seemed. And remembering how God had tested His people by marching them in the wilderness, *to prove thee, to know what was in thine heart, whether thou wouldest keep his commandments*—remembering that, a pious sense of emulation had made Smith do an extraordinary thing. He had joined the American army, experimentally he had chosen the sword instead of the shepherd's crook. He believed that if his faith survived, if his flesh turned cold at the instruments of death, his trigger-finger impotent, if Vietnam itself couldn't make him break God's holy law *thou shalt not kill*—if the red in him yielded to the black then he could be certain of God's intent, the neck he was bravely sticking out should wear a clergyman's collar.

Palefaced, his glassy spectacles managing to reflect a light bulb at all times, the eyes behind it those of a worried boy on a railway train that he *thinks* is right, Smith had taken his basic training at this same camp before he had gone to further training at M. One morning in autumn, Smith had attached a thin piece of steel to his Army rifle to be taught bayonet by a sergeant who knew the secret of man against man: that victory goes to the spirited, not to the strong or the skilled. "So when I say *what is the purpose of the h*

...₁...₁'s

...₁...₁₅ overdid it in Franken-
...₁ meets-the-Wolfman fashion, *aargh!* one or two
delinquents serious about it but nobody else.

"You're getting better," the sergeant declared—
but Smith hadn't spoken a blessed word, Smith was
bereft of tongue. And when the sergeant took these
chortling soldiers into the bayonet's maniacal reper-
tory—*on guard—vertical butt-stroke and hold—
smash—slash—on guard*—try though he might,
Smith couldn't join in this horseplay, instead he did
every angular movement in a very namby-pamby
manner. At last the tough old drill sergeant took him
aside. A man whose honorable mission was nothing
but to save Smith's life at the expense of those who
wouldn't spare it, the sergeant told him in disap-
pointment to try—simply try.

Now, Smith was no seminarian. Religion to him
wasn't a fair cosmology as round as a crystal ball but
a sort of Chinese puzzle, he still hadn't fitted it together, some of the pretty blue and white plastic
pieces might not even belong. But that Christianity
was a colloquy, Smith understood—that as God di-
vulged his wishes to man through visions, so man
disclosed his worries to God through prayers. And
that night kneeling at his Army bed and praying in
sibilant whispers, to Smith it was only natural to
add to his usual inventory, "And Father, I didn't
have the spirit with the bayonet today. Father, may
it be Thy will to help me with the bayonet." The next

day Smith's prayer was answered, Smith felt the will of God working through his lunging arms to the very tip of the shining steel, *He teacheth my hands to war,* and Smith was able to cry *to kill* from the very bottom of his heart.

Smith's second crisis came on the rifle range, his chest in the frozen sand, his cheek on the oily stock of his automatic rifle, his spectacled right eye on a pale cardboard target. No little Euclidean bull's-eye, his bullet's destination was a piece of cardboard in a man's silhouette, head on his broad shoulders, hits and misses were the Army's only scores. *Ready on the left! Ready on the right! Ready on the firing line! Commence . . . fire!* but Smith couldn't fire, arthritis seemed to have seized his trigger-finger, it was a sun-dried bone. Smith scored a fat round zero and that night he prayed again. "Father," he said, "I didn't qualify in my M14A2 today. Father, grant that I may qualify in this weapon." And qualify Smith did, the felt breath of God loosened his paralyzed muscle and Smith won a sharpshooter's medal his second time round. *And the Spirit of the Lord came mightily upon him, and the cords that were upon his arms became as flax that was burnt with fire, and [he] slew a thousand men.*

Pride: the first of the deadly sins. But still, Smith can be forgiven for telling himself as basic training came to its rough-and-tumble end, *I've done myself proud—I've been two months in the Army and I've not given in, I'm still the worker of God's will.* But even as Smith congratulated himself on the viability of his Christian faith, he sensed a little rift of discontinuity on the happy plateau of his thoughts: it was as though two of his lovely blue and white beliefs didn't want to interconnect. And tenderly lifting them to study them as a lepidopterist might with a pair of perfect fritillaries, a paradox presented itself to Smith's startled eyes. He became aware that the

... goes, *and where it stops no mortal knows,* but Smith didn't dare to look at his dilemma's darkest center, the ultimate induction that if every bit of foolery could call itself God's will as long as man's prayer preceded it the night before—then God's bonafide will could never be known and Smith was a mariner with no bright steadfast star. And so Smith's spirit had descended into the black night of the soul even as Smith's flesh was being graduated into Mighty Mike.

Of course, Smith had gone to the Chaplain. But that worthy shepherd cared for a flock whose agonies weren't existential and weren't beyond the reach of a gentle pastoral pat. The Protestant major expected to hear soldiers say, "I don't like the chow," or "I don't want to kill people," and he had rehearsed himself to throw back his head and answer merrily, "Well! Welcome to the club!" But he wasn't prepared for Jesuitical searches into the whereabouts of God's intent.

It was to this limited man's businesslike chapel that our Dostoevskian character came on a fall afternoon, his soul like a twisted wet towel. Eight totally naked ladies stood in the vestibule and didn't say "Eek" as Smith hurried by, unaware of their round breasts or their androgynous goatees. A set of old Macy's manikins, the Chaplain had acquired them to resurrect them as a Christmas nativity scene: we three kings of Orient, the same number of certain poor shepherds, round yon virgin mother, and Joseph. The major himself was a formidable soldier of God, as Smith could perceive when he sat down opposite him at his oaken desk. Like the apical star on a Christmas tree, the little silver cross on the Chaplain's green collar crowned a life's accumulation of bright decorations: a combat infantryman's silver rifle and four glorious rows of ribbons led by the bronze star for valor with three oakleaf clusters, to signify that the Chaplain had earned it again and again and again. He listened as Smith began about the sergeant saying to everyone, *what is the purpose of the bayonet? to kill* and—

Stop. There wasn't a day that a worried recruit didn't come to the Chaplain's office with a question beginning and ending in those same hesitant words. *"Well,"* the Chaplain laughed, "the sergeant isn't saying kill as in *kill.* This is just to build up spirit, kill the umpire sort of thing. You've been to ball games, yes?"

"Yes . . ." His spectacles reflecting the dying daylight in the company areas, Smith tried to think. A vague intimation of relevance appeared to adhere to the Chaplain's item of information, and Smith sought to fit it into the recent disappearance of God's will. Somehow it wouldn't fit.

"Or how about this," the Chaplain was saying. "If a man's standing there with a bayonet to your throat—well, wouldn't you try to defend yourself?"

"Sir, I don't know," Smith replied and he kept up his effort to think—think—think. "I might just maybe say *Father forgive him.* It tells us thou shalt not kill."

"Oh, that's not a good translation," the Chaplain said. "It's really thou shalt not murder. Remember that Joshua killed. And Samson did, and *Saul hath slain his thousands and David his ten thousands.* And don't forget St. Paul. He remember said be a good soldier . . ." and as the Chaplain talked on, fur-

...read their intricate replies, he rose at the Chaplain's prayer meetings to ask that everyone sing *I need Thee, oh I need Thee.* This winter's morning he sat in the vast classroom waiting for another revelation as the Chaplain pushed his pulpit across the linoleum and said in his inspiring voice, "Courage! Courage is not something we are born with, it is not handed out in the supply room, it is not a piece of equipment, it is not . . ."

But at this instant there was a very important event a hundred miles away. And had M only known what a fragile vessel all of its hopes reposed in that morning, its thoughts would have leapt from the Chaplain's lecture and fled across the intervening states to settle on, *tarantara* . . . the Chillicothe milkman! His name was Elmer Pulver. His was the route east of the N&W tracks in Chillicothe, Ohio, in 1950, when the Korean war began. Elmer in his creaky horse-drawn cart, bringing in newspapers from the gate, rapping on the door cheerily, tat-a-tat-*tat,* closing the gate behind him so the dog couldn't get out, the nicest, most up-and-coming milkman in town, giving little tasty chips of ice to the very same children who'd be draft-eligible when he was a major in the US Army in Washington, in 1966. Pulver was called up in 1951, but he chose going to Officer Candidate School. Having asked for the infantry first, tanks second, artillery third, he was granted none of these, and as a young lieutenant of engineers he asked for Korea but was flown off to Germany—ah, the whimsical *they!* By 1966, Pulver, now a major and still terribly nice, had been given a desk in the Pentagon's windowless inner rings, also an old wooden swivel chair and a new task: every (no exaggeration, *every*) man in the Army, after he was through training would be assigned to a duty station by Major Pulver. Far from being three horrid witches out on a heath somewhere dancing around a pot, *they* would be Elmer Pulver.

This winter morning he had a stack of those stiff IBM cards the size of an old British pound note, one apiece for every soldier in M. The cards had green edges, and Pulver had a second deck of colorless IBM cards, one apiece for everywhere on this earth that the Army had an opening for a rifleman. Seated at his swivel chair, Pulver now took a corncob from its round rack, filled it with tobacco, lit it, and started fingering through his IBMs. Doing it the Army way, he would need to take absolutely any green card and white card and fasten them together with a paper clip: rifleman and assignment and on to the next, another day, another dollar. But the Major was a nice person; he knew he had human beings of many kidneys there in his busy fingers and though it meant working overtime—today was a Saturday, the Pentagon was strange and empty—he wanted to put each soldier where he'd be happiest. And on each boy's IBM card there was a code letter signifying where on this varied planet he would honestly hope to be stationed next.

Some of M wanted the *dolce vita* in Europe. Some had opted for sunny Hawaii or the Caribbean's warm waters. A few adventurous souls had elected: Japan. Were the IBM cards to be believed, none of

earn $65 a month combat pay, which he figured
would add to $780 after his twelve months' tour of
duty. This he figured to put into IBM: where, he figured, in a few thrifty years it would appreciate to
$1000, which—but beyond that Bigalow hadn't fig-
ured. But thus far in his Army career, Bigalow
hadn't made his preference known to the proper authorities, no fault of Bigalow's. Many nights earlier,
a tall PFC from the personnel office had gathered M
in its dayroom—a rumpus room, an area whose
bright green pool and ping-pong tables a soldier saw
whenever he was assigned to shine the linoleum beneath them; otherwise it was kept behind a steel
chain, off limits. That night, though, it had been
opened extraordinarily to let that PFC give everyone
some little gray mimeographed forms. "Awright!"
he had said. "Now, those who would like to go to
Europe write down, *Europe,*" no promises made. He
himself had taken one mimeographed form and
curled it around his index finger, and while he spoke
he wiggled it like a swizzlestick in a highball glass or
a pencil making *O*'s: a gesture that might have
meant the Army's having its people eternally fill in
mimeographed forms. In fact, M had filled in forms
so habitually that within minutes it would forget forever ever having completed *these.* "Awright," said
PFC Swizzlestick. "Those who want the Caribbean . . ." and similarly for Alaska, Hawaii, Japan,
Korea, Okinawa, and Bigalow's coveted Vietnam.

Then he had gathered up the mimeographed papers and cabled them to the Pentagon, but Bigalow was on KP that evening, standing in white clouds of steam and washing pans. So the code letter on his green IBM card was an X, meaning no known preference.

Puffing his corncob and thumbing through his second deck of cards, Pulver now learned that in one month the Army had vacancies in Germany and in Vietnam—no place else. Now it happened this freezing Saturday that he had brought his blond and eight-year-old son, Douglas, to the Pentagon (in a week it was Lisa's turn) and to satisfy Douglas's curiosity he showed him the IBM cards, explaining that a soldier who wanted to go to Europe really would and a soldier would go to Vietnam who wanted to—though apparently none did. "Supposing he wants to go to Japan?" Douglas alertly asked, and Pulver explained that though there were no openings that month in this pretty land of geisha girls and cherry blossoms, though there were no Japanese slots he would do his level best by that soldier and order him to Vietnam, since he seemed interested in the Orient and could stop in Japan itself, perhaps, going over or coming back. "Supposing he wants, Hawaii?" Douglas said, and Pulver replied: the same, he would go to Vietnam. "Daddy! I can do it myself—*please,*" Douglas said, but Daddy chuckled and said no, and as Douglas sat across from him with a set of crayons drawing some colorful jet airplanes his father began to clip cards together, the green and the white. At noon Douglas ate a hamburger at his desk, Pulver had a roast-beef sandwich on white bread at his.

At noon an apprehensive M waited in its tidy barracks for Captain Amaker's arrival. Amaker, though, was innocently upon the turnpike in his white Triumph convertible gaily driving to New

studios of

photographers. Instead, M would
have its adequacy appraised by that fox in sheep's
clothing, Sergeant Machiavelli—Milett. He started
inspecting the barracks at 2 o'clock. He wasn't in
any very aggravated mood until a moment later,
when his fingers moved across the very first soldier's
footlocker so as to open it. And then Milett recognized from the almost imperceptible impedance that
it gave to his fingertips the presence of that loath-
some substance to whose annihilation he had de-
voted much of his Army career. He cried out *"Dust!"*
and stretching his fingers wide enough to hold a basketball he pushed them at the face of the footlocker's
unfortunate owner, whose name was Private Scott.
"Goddam! This is a shame," Milett cried, and Scotty
looked truly contrite, eyes on the floor. Usually he
was a fun-loving guy, a Negro. The day before Swizzlestick's poll he had watched *Hawaiian Eye* on television, and on the mimeographed questionnaire he
had written, "Hawaii," so that he could dance with
the lulu girls.

   "Dust!. . . *Dust!*. . . *Dust!*. . . *All of them!"* Milett
said, hurling himself from locker to locker and giving each the fingertip test, a furious Pancho
Gonzalez forehand. *"This is a court-martial offense!*
You aren't ready for inspection!" he screamed—and
suddenly his face wasn't purple, his skin wasn't
bedsheet tight, the sergeant was no longer angry. He
laughed. He had realized, this whole thing was

ridiculous—ridiculous, that a man should present himself for inspection with his footlocker dusty. "You people . . . you people," laughing, taking his handkerchief out, wiping the filth from his fingers. "You better wake up, you people don't wake up now you'll never wake up. Only with a bad-conduct discharge. And," his head shaking incredulously, "this is just a sergeant's inspection, suppose it had been the Captain himself!" *Cap*-tain-him-self is how he pronounced it; quick little quarter-notes. Milett was a Puerto Rican. Three times, the Caribbean had knocked down the house where he'd grown up; immigrating to Harlem, shining people's shoes so he could take his girl to the movie but worrying *what if she sees me shining shoes,* washing his hands with Borax but thinking *if I touch her maybe she'll smell it*—ten years, and then he had found the Army, where a life to be proud of lay within a man's aspirations: even a Puerto Rican's. He said to M now, "I was a PFC," pronouncing it *pee*-eff-see. "When the officer opened my locker he had to use sunglasses! because I didn't have a towel there, I had aluminum foil all around! And the man said to me, *You're going to make it some day."* Milett's eyes shone as he remembered, there was silverfoil behind his irises. What he couldn't reconcile himself to and couldn't forgive was that M didn't have initiative—M didn't really *care.*

His punishment: no passes that Saturday afternoon. With those melancholy words Milett went to his rooms on the Army post, where he told the day's happenings to his sexy, sweater-wearing wife, showing her the tainted handkerchief. Demirgian and most people went to sleep on their brown Army blankets. At the Pentagon, Pulver finished his work, and after driving Douglas home he took the family's beagle, Socks, to the veterinarian's who gave it shots

⊔⊔ ᴛʜɪɴᴋɪɴɢ . . . *almost* . . . *almost*. On center stage in their spangled dresses the Barnes sisters did their little dance, and Prochaska, one of M's few emissaries on the club's folding seats, sang quietly along, tapping his visored hat against one knee. "Oh, I hate to see-e-e . . ." At 7 that evening Milett had given M its passes—but Prochaska couldn't leave, he didn't have the money, they hadn't paid him in months. Something was wrong at the finance office.

Well . . . that's all right, Prochaska thought. He was happy singing, and he thought that the Barnes sisters were two really good-looking girls. A pity—he would have liked to buy them hamburgers after the show, but Shirley and Wanda had other enlisted men's clubs to do their little dance at. Prochaska had supper without them but that's all right, he thought—he liked eating hamburgers. Prochaska liked everything, really. He liked turning over the soil on his family's Iowa cornfield, he liked going camping in Minnesota, canoeing on the soda-water rivers and smelling the fish frying at night. Had he believed more in religion he would have thanked God for these bounties, but he believed in his country and that is what Prochaska thanked. Grateful to America he had joined the Army as other men might tithe to their church. He was eighteen years old; still, one could imagine his honest face and thin-rimmed spectacles engraved on some friendly curlicued bottle label, some liniment that all the folk in the county swore by, Old Doc Prochaska's Tonic.

In a word, he was a soldier who in mediocre war novels would die in the next chapter to last. Prochaska knew that he could be killed in Vietnam but he told himself—eating alone in the dark Paradise restaurant just off post, drinking a Coke from a glass, the jukebox strumming a song about a lonely soldier writing his mother from Vietnam itself—he told himself, that's all right, better me than someone with a wife or a family. His mother was already dead; one winter morning, lighting a stove in their Iowa farmhouse, not knowing that the chimney was choked with ice, she had been wounded fatally when the stove exploded and his father had been burned, half a year in the hospital. Prochaska was seven then. He had been prescient about this—he had dreamt of it three nights earlier. Prochaska had presciences often.

The song on the jukebox was to become Prochaska's favorite:

My dearest mama, they just gave us time to write,
I miss you and there's something on my mind
  tonight,
At mail call I received your letter here today,
But I don't understand the things you say.

You tell me there are people marching in our
  streets,

Prochaska knew about them. On his Christmas vacation he and a tall pleasant buddy, Morton by name, had gone to New York City, where a lady in Times Square had given them leaflets saying we were strafing the Asian countryside, killing the men, women, and children. Another leaflet of hers purported to show a little Cambodian girl burned by

them at his target. He thought now, *I've got a high score, I've qualified to go to Vietnam.* He put another dime in the flashy jukebox, playing his song again.

It became colder. M was on maneuvers now. This meant living in tents and tearing about on four square miles of mock battlefields mornings, afternoons, and evenings, guns at the ready, helmets on, learning how to acquit itself in the enemy's presence. And this meant—ugh! getting dirt on its combat boots, it meant acquiring water-drops in its canteens and hard round flecks of coagulated gravy in its messkits, it meant in its *rifles!* a residue of carbon-like matter, this and just twenty-four hours after M would finish maneuvering, back in its dusty barracks with all this execrable stuff, the Major himself would inspect it.

"I wouldn't worry—he shouldn't be bad," Prochaska was telling guys, "a major hasn't the time," untrue. For even as M settled into its cold foxholes its captain stood slightly aside on the battlefield saying uh-huh . . . uh-huh as the Major enumerated his expectations, *cap à pied.* He told him, "The first thing is the brass," meaning the little yellow U.S. buttons, "I want 'em five-eighths of an inch," meaning from the collar's edge, "I'm really tight on that. Then—the necktie," simulating on his blue infantry scarf, "it should be up real tight. Then going down. The rifleman's medal—is it centered? The pocket buttons . . ." His name was Major Small. A good officer, a veteran of Vietnam, well liked by his soldiers, his tragedy was to be at that uncertain stage in his Army career when, no longer a captain, he wasn't yet a lieutenant colonel, he had nothing to do but command a battalion—that is, nothing to do. His

scribbling, "I am sure if I went into any area I would sooner or later find people taking a break from the rigors of their diurnal duties," and then he had scrawled, *"Res Ipsa Loquitur,"* hoping the Major had to look it up. Unlike President Lincoln, the Irish lieutenant had really fired his letter off, though he routed it through a chain of command that he knew would shudder and fire it back before it could settle *s-s-s-s* on the Major's desk.

Better a sabbatical in Torremolinos, waiting out the lieutenant colonelcy list and writing the *Memoirs of a Company-Grade Officer.* But regulations forbade it. ". . . All right," the Major was saying, "on down. Are the boots polished?" the Major touching abruptly on rock bottom, giving M's captain a parting wink, and, after pausing to tell a private to shave, quitting the field.

By then, M was in its foxholes and waiting to be mock attacked. The sky was the color of factory fumes and under it the empty battlefield stretched and stretched, it seemed a man might need a month to cross it, crows would be the only living creatures. M had some blank ammunition in its cold rifles, and after expending this it had orders to cry *bang! bang! bang!* enthusiastically. The young lieutenant, whose attaboy way of talking would make him an excellent boy scout counselor in civilian life, though he was an insurance salesman, was jogging from one bleak foxhole to another, giving each man a love-tap on his helmet, urging him on. "Hey there!" he said to Scotty, of the dusty footlocker. "I've got your position spotted—know why? Your messkit! I could hear it rattling 'way off. Fill it with something!" the lieutenant said. "Fill it with leaves—pine needles—a pair of mitten liners—newspaper—toilet paper—cotton—old powder puffs," he seemed to be saying, "ticker tape—feathers," and Scotty paid attention, trying to remember everything that the lieutenant was telling him to fill his messkit with so it wouldn't rattle. The lieutenant gave him a love-tap and moved to another Negro soldier, who appeared to have frozen to death inside his foxhole. "Hey, young man—are you cold?" he asked.

"Yes, sir," words from the grave.

"Where are you from?"

"Newark, sir."

"Well, weren't you this cold playing b-ball?"

"What, sir?"

"Playing basketball?"

"No, sir."

"Well—weren't you out in the streets?"

"No, sir, we were in the gym."

"Well—weren't you in the streets sometimes?"

"In the summer, sir."

The lieutenant shrugged, and giving him no tap he moved on to Williams, also a Negro, a simple Florida boy whose imagination was always getting jerked out of its innocence whenever the Army spelled out to its soldiers what it expected of them. "Attaboy—keep yourself down in the foxhole. Nothing above it," said the lieutenant. "Only your head."

Only my head. Are they serious? Williams said to himself. Could it be, that of his body's he-didn't-know-how-many bones the Army would have him expose the very one that was most sensitive to enemy fire? Were common sense and soldiering so alien, then? A hand or an elbow, now—if duty required it,

...around Florida spying on his three little brothers and three little sisters, none of them the wiser. A periscope could be fitted to his rifle sight, the rifle could be held above his foxhole—*hmm.* Williams thought about this as the mock enemy army attacked, as a Choctaw Indian sergeant shouted through a loudspeaker, *"Americans—surrender!* You don't surrender we'll cut off your fingers!"

That day at lunch, Williams talked periscopes with a more sophisticated Philadelphia friend of his, Hofelder, both of them sitting on the frosted battlefield. In their narrow messkits the pale vegetables were merging into one another like watercolors. Except for its tasting cold, the lunch was no better or worse than M's usual diet—at this moment, actually, give or take adjustments for time zones, the whole American army was being served the same thing, the master menu it was called. Williams and Hofelder were eating this master menu except that at M the apples in the fruit salad had been deleted and bananas had been substituted, when Williams broached his revolutionary idea.

"Yeah, but you could just see in front of you," Hofelder said. "You couldn't see on your flanks."

"Well . . . ," said Williams.

"There's no sense looking in front if they're going to jump in your foxhole behind."

"Well . . . maybe it wouldn't work. But maybe it would," said Williams.

"They gave me one of those things, I wouldn't use it I'd throw it away."

"Well . . . it might not be good. But it might not be bad," said Williams, thoughtfully chewing his pan-fried liver.

In the distance they could hear little Swiss cowbells tinkling—actually it was soldiers finishing chow and washing their messkits in the steaming cans. In the afternoon M had more maneuvers, offense not defense and a different lieutenant—oh my God, a different lieutenant! No gay sideline cheers like *attaboy* or *attaway to do it* loosened the tight lips of Second Lieutenant Chorba, in Chorba's clenched fingers there were no little fluttering love-taps awaiting their birth. For within Chorba's breast there sat an apprehension of imminent catastrophe, a sense of M's ineludible doom had twisted itself around his heart and under it the joyous things of his life lay bluish-black, a strangled bird. The cause of this knotted despondency was Chorba's knowledge that in three inevitable minutes *(tick . . . tick . . . tick . . .)* when M company walked across this battlefield in a mock attack its personnel would be firing real ammunition.

Angels and ministers of grace defend us! Three thousand pieces of solid lead to be sent shrieking above America at four times the speed of sound, seventeen billion ergs of energy in each irresponsible one of them, and each of them instantaneously activated at the flick of an adolescent's finger. Merciful God! What cataclysmic threat to America's security could have misled the Pentagon to such an insane experiment, what cursed spite had wished it on Chorba's head to have to preside! *Everything insofar as it is in itself endeavors to persist in its own being—* Spinoza had written that and Chorba once wouldn't have denied it, *I believe it* he would have declared until he became the safety officer on M's practice bat-

... afternoon this wretched lieutenant awaited the hour of attack by marshaling all of the screaming meemies within him, all his blood transubstantiated to choler and undiluted dudgeon rose in his gorge until his whole tongue was awash in it. Whenever he muttered to himself it seemed to be with a mouthful of chili con carne.

Five. Four. Three. Two. One. *Ignition,* and as M went over the top firing from its waddling hips and shouting its *aargh . . . aargh . . . aargh,* all of Chorba's purple juices rose in his system, they passed through the narrow nozzle of his neck and emerged from his skull like the shriek of a factory whistle. *"Jesus, trainee,"* he cried to a boy whose aggressiveness had taken him well ahead of the line of fire. "Where are your brains? Do you want to get killed? Do you like being dead? Jesus! Get yourself back in line! *Dammit,* trainee," to a boy whose rifle sat in his hands like a bone in a spaniel's paws, "is there something the matter with you? Are you crazy or something? Get all your goddam mittens off! *Jesus,"* to a boy whose rifle looked like a little umbrella, its muzzle had exploded open, "do you want to wake up dead? Did you ever clean that piece of yours? *Dammit!* Are you tired of living, trainee," to a boy whose automatic rifle had caught on some brambles and swung around, the muzzle was in his stomach, "do you want to die or something? *Oh! Oh! Jesus Christ!"* Chorba exclaimed. Because far on the right flank of M, Hofelder, the bony Philadelphia soldier who didn't care for periscopes, was still in his foxhole fiddling with his trigger mechanism while his countrymen moved ahead of his unpredictable rifle—the rifle was momentarily jammed. *"Oh Jesus Christ! Trainee, do you have brains in your feet? Do you have rocks in your head? Move out!"*

"Sir, the rifle is—" Hofelder pleasantly began, but he was like someone spitting into a hurricane.

"Dammit, trainee! Were you born yesterday? Don't you understand orders? Move out!" Roger, and Hofelder moved so alacritously that in five quick seconds he himself was in front of somebody's smoking rifle. *"Jesus, trainee, use your brains! This way! This way,"* Chorba screamed to him from behind his imperiled back.

"Lieutenant sir? Which way?" Hofelder asked, and he turned around for a *this way* or *that way,* a movement that had a collateral effect of directing his unreliable rifle at Chorba's recoiling chest.

"Oh JESUS—JESUS—JESUS—JESUS—" Chorba cried, and his whole personality disintegrated, his arms and his legs detached themselves from their sockets and sailed across the battlefield like Olympic hammers, his torso fell to the field like a bagged Canada goose, it melted into a pool of butter and Chorba hasn't been heard from since. His sacrifice wasn't in vain, though. M achieved the opposite end of its battlefield without a one of its trainees wounded or dead—though it wasn't to end these maneuvers until a boy who didn't know it was loaded had fired a one-gun salute two or three inches from Prochaska's unprepared neck.

For supper M ate a master menu in which the chocolate cream pie had been deleted and chocolate cake had been substituted, one squinting diner missing his little messkit in the twilight and eating a cold spoonful of substituted sand. The company

mented soldier whom God's will might or might not have intended for the pulpit.

"Oh? But the Lord recognizes war?"

"Let me say this," Smith replied, "the Lord is with us everywhere, even on the battlefield. He that lives by the sword shall die by the sword." A few more moments of thought revealed to Smith that if his first precept was of doubtful pertinence his second citation couldn't apply less, and he lapsed into introspective silence while he chewed on his buttered green beans.

. . . *Tinkle, tinkle, steaming can, wash the silver, rinse the pan.* At night M had more maneuverings: defense again, the winter air as cold as a butcher's cleaver, the stars like a bed of nails, the voice of the Choctaw calling, "Surrender, Americans! We have a nice warm fire here, nice and warm . . . ," and M in its icy foxholes aching to fire its rifles to thaw its fingers on the tepid barrels. Until with a pinched little cry of *yippee* another long day of maneuvers came to its cold close.

But even before taps was to play totally inaudibly from the adjutant's office a good twenty miles away and a whimsical private was to sing, *"Good night, ladies . . . good night, ladies . . . ,"* a curious circumstance was to fit this parenthetical day into time's continuum, a most significant topic of talk would arise in Williams's and Hofelder's cold squad tent and briefly insinuate itself amidst the more usual ones. It was *Vietnam,* and it cropped up almost naturally. M had gotten back at 9 o'clock; now, huddling stiffly over a pot-bellied stove, the wind blowing the bare electric light bulb crazily about, his shadow skittering over the dirt floor, a soldier from Texas had muttered, "Close the door," as somebody else walked in. "Were you born in a barn?"

And a second soldier had said, "He was born in a cave. That's why he leaves the door open."

And a third soldier had said, *"Now* it's so cold, for twelve months we'll be where it's a hundred degrees at night."

And that was it, the topic would seldom rise again throughout maneuvers, Vietnam was far in the future—weeks. The last words of this conversation would be Yoshioka's, a boy born in California of Japanese parents who almost never wrote to him or telephoned him, a boy of heavy spirit who'd had it on good authority (a sergeant's) that the Army didn't send Orientals to this Asian war because the other soldiers might fire at them mistakenly. Yoshioka now said, "Shit," his favorite figure of speech, an idiom that in Yoshioka's voice slid by degrees down the scale and curled itself back on itself like a scorpion's tail or the corners of Yoshioka's mouth. "I'm not going to be there—I'm an Oriental," he announced, and then people talked of the cold again.

Needless to say, Yoshioka had answered Swizzlestick's questionnaire by asking to go to Japan—he had a grandmother there. Williams had asked for Europe, none of those dangerous foxholes, and Hofelder had been on KP.

Demirgian thought *no! no no no!* they could torture him, court-martial him, *ta-ta-ta-ta* the firing squad, anything! but *I'm . . . not . . . getting . . . a haircut! No!* His buddies were coming in from the

policy there was no roughing a trooper and *surely* no wrenching his wallet away and giving the barber his seventy-five cents, union scale. Demirgian hurling himself free, the barber was poorer by a fourth of his minute-by-minute wages when he drove his Cadillac from the post, whose general himself had muttered once, "*I* should be in that business."

The thing had been a sergeant's idea—the haircuts. With the Major inspecting M tomorrow, with the footlockers parallel, the toilet articles in each of them congruent with the next's, *still* the sergeant had known that his sense of symmetry would be betrayed by those uncontrolled towers of protoplasm who would stand by the very aisles the Major would walk through—some of them brachycephalic, some of them prognathic, some of them different *colors*. Cosmetic surgery being ridiculous, at least he could order M into one harmonious state of bald-headedness. Demirgian knew—he would stick out tomorrow like a porcupine in a pumpkin patch, he foresaw that, he imagined the Major coming to him saying, "Soldier, don't you know to take off your hair in an officer's presence?" or something as withering, eyeing him coldly. If that happened Demirgian thought he couldn't contain himself, him an individualist, an Armenian, he thought he would scream terrible things at the Major, his heart sank as he saw himself tearing his uniform off, throwing his combat stuff to the floor, dumping his footlocker over . . .

. . . *Why not?* If that didn't get him out of the Army, would anything do it? Demirgian thought. And so the next morning Demirgian stood at his green footlocker steeling himself against the Major's fateful question, determined to follow his natural bent.

Truth to tell, the Major himself didn't look forward to inspecting M, it would be a distasteful duty. For every soldier he came to was meant to bring his rifle to the crisp position of inspection arms, saying, "Sir! Private so-and-so, such-and-such platoon," and M being what it was . . . well. When the Major started with Scotty everything went smoothly, Scotty was easygoing, but as he came to the second footlocker the soldier there absolutely shouted, *"Sir! Private Pender! Third platoon!"* and covered the Major with little drops of water that had to remain there—for as inspecting officer, dressed in his Army greens, his campaign ribbons a rainbow, the Major thought it would be ludicrous if he were constantly seen to be wiping his face with his handkerchief. "You don't have to sound off quite so loudly," he said to Pender, who happened to be the camp's heavyweight boxing champion, "try it conversationally," but he had two hundred and fifty more soldiers to go. At length he came to a boy whose contorted face, an iron boiler almost ready to pop, promised an even lustier reception than most. Resignedly the Major stood there—but Demirgian was waiting too, waiting for the Major's hair-raising reprimand. Whole geologic eras seemed to pass, canyons eroded, the dinosaurs became extinct, until one of the parties to this awful silence finally broke it, whispering, *"My* name is Major Small."

Taken unawares, Demirgian said, *"Uh . . ."* and then he said, "Sir . . . Private Demirgian."

"Try to remember to say that," the Major said and

ııs sunny office and, opening the manila envelope, actually turned pale. He ran through the names by leaps and bounds and after putting them in again, closing the envelope quickly, twisting the little red string around those two brown cardboard buttons, shoving everything into a desk drawer, locking it, and pocketing the little key, he reflected that he couldn't keep his awful secret forever, that there'd be a day of reckoning when M must be told—by him, First Sergeant Doherty. He knew about lost battalions, the Japanese death marches, the charges of light brigades, one didn't become a soldier without understanding that there'd be— *times,* but never had Doherty's own career been touched by tragedy so closely as now. He said to himself, if only—*if only I had some good news to give them, as well!* just as your family doctor might say you've got asthma—now you can live in Arizona. And then there arose in the reaches of Doherty's mind the dawn of an extraordinary idea. Something that he himself could do for M's unfortunate boys, and hurrying to the next sunny office he said "Sir . . ." and he broached his thought to the Captain—who, though he admired it, saying it wasn't within his authority to approve, brought it up with the Major—who, with a heartfelt I-would-if-I-could, channeled it to the Colonel—who cautiously routed it to the General but recommended its ratification: while at the bottom of this mighty pyramid, Doherty waited and waited, his high hopes tempered by knowing that no first sergeant in this camp's history had ever managed to do this fantastic thing.

Meanwhile . . . the General had other business. What he gave priority to was that infantry classes be more effective, and calling his trim colonels and majors to Doughboy Hall he lectured them on what he meant *effective,* this is General Ekman. He said, a classroom isn't the place for a hut! two! three! four! stomach in! chest out! sergeant—no, in there a sergeant should be relaxed, colloquial, he should use gestures to make his point, similes from baseball, basketball, anything if it works. "Look at me—I have my hands in my pocket," the General said, barely suppressing a smile. "Is there any man who can't understand me because of my hands in my pocket? If *so,*" with a wink, "I'm going to take them out," and the colonels and majors chuckled, getting the point. Back at their desks, they paraphrased this to their captains, who simplified it for their lieutenants, until when the sergeants who actually taught these infantry classes drank at this bucket of Pierian wisdom only a drop remained: be more effective. This the husky sergeants interpreted to mean stand at attention and shout even louder. "Let us!" the Choctaw Indian sergeant would say, standing as stiff as a cannon barrel—"Let us begin by! osserving! the lines a this map!" his neck almost paralyzed, "here is . . . correction! *here!* is the prow liner ploint!" for who can stand at attention shouting *the probable line of deployment* with his stomach sucked in, the ferocious sergeant style?

But there was a sergeant who dared to be natural—a Sergeant Foley. Forty years old, bald-headed, an Irish story-teller sort of guy, whenever of-

out in front

was this *little— tiny—* evergreen tree.
But when morning came it was just an ever-tree because he was so scared of it, he'd shot off all the
green!" Obviously, Foley was the Mr. Dooley of
Army sergeants.

This snowy day in the windy Klondike shack that
was Foley's classroom, he was teaching M something
important—going on night patrols. "Now if you're
going out to infiltrate a quartermaster laundry company," he began, smiling but serious, "well . . . you
can take flashlights along. But if you're going to another rifle company you'll want to be careful, you'll
take advantage of *every— little—* lousy thing there
is," unpleasant for Foley to say, worse for M not to
have heard. "If your rifle doesn't work, are you going
to stand there with a finger up? You do, you know
how you're coming back to the States. In a wooden
overcoat. If you haven't anything else to hit Charlie
with," Charlie being our enemy in this war, Victor
Charlie, the VC, *"stick— your— thumb— right in his
eyes and push it to the back of his head!"* Foley gave
his instructions with a rueful September smile—for
it was ludicrous, two people who hadn't been intro-
duced gouging each other's eyes out, Swift would
have thought so, Brecht, but Foley didn't start this
war, he only taught about it. "That's the way to take
care of those people. Grab 'em by the balls, if *you're*
grabbing *them* you're going to feel no pain."

Seated on a cold classroom bench, one of Foley's

pupils hung on his every diabolical word: Russo his name was. Small and round and wild-eyed, the Quixotic victim of too many late-late shows on television, Russo had suddenly lied and joined the Army when he was sixteen, and he sat whispering heroic things like *"Aargh!"* as Foley spoke. But behind Russo two older soldiers played tic-tac-toe and a third whispered, "I got winners." Demirgian's friend Sullivan toyed with his rifle-repair tool, musing, *this could be a deadly weapon. Crack-k-k! Put someone's eye out!* Standing up not sitting down, Prochaska was keeping the sandman at bay after a night of walking in circles in a military manner, mounting guard, and another boy from guard duty now slowly sensed that a rifle-repair tool was jabbing him in the ribs as Sullivan told him, *"Wake up,"* Sullivan had had guard duty too. Demirgian—guard duty too—leaned over his spiral notebook drawing a long zigzag line, his ball-point pen never leaving the paper: a style of art he had arrived at at twelve, independently of Paul Klee. First he drew a caret mark, $\wedge$, and bridging them he drew another $\wedge$ beneath it, until his small stack of $\wedge$s began to resolve themselves into a sergeant's chevrons. Around them, Demirgian's unrelenting pen delineated an arm, with hairpin turns it made fingers, it curved over a hairless head, dropped into a hideous smile, and after pursuing its wayward course down to a belly it manifested itself as a pair of legs, terminating on the left combat boot—whereupon, Demirgian saw he had left something out. Again putting pen to paper, Demirgian wrote on the sleeve where the service stripes go, the word DUMB.

"That's all one line," he whispered, letting Sullivan see it.

"One line?" and tracing it with his finger, "Yeah . . . it's all one line. Captain?"

"Sergeant!" said Demirgian, his feelings hurt.

specting his footlocker, telling him to pick up matches and clean his boots—anyplace was better than M, anyhow it wouldn't be cold. Still . . . there were other romantic places, and when Swizzlestick had polled him Demirgian had written, "Europe" on one of those mimeographed forms, "Caribbean" on another, and "Korea" on a third, he wasn't taking chances.

—Up front, Foley and his night patrol were in the attack. *"Go on*—you're firing from the hip, if somebody's in a hole, he throws a grenade, *go down in the hole with him!* that's what you've got that knife on the end of your rifle for!"

"Aargh! Fix bayonets!" Russo yelled under his breath.

"Then— you— leave— and get lost in the woods just as fast as you can. Because old Charlie is going to be after you!"

"He looks like a homo," Sullivan whispered to a friend.

"Just because he looks like your father. . . ."

"How's your wife and my kids?" Sullivan whispered.

His lecture over, Foley put a technicolor movie on, whose narrator also talked straight from the shoulder. He said, "I'm Sergeant Crowley and I'm taking out a night patrol," and he said, I'm getting my men ready, they're putting on camouflage, I'm giving them mud and dirt and ashes and burnt cork, they're rubbing it onto their boots, their clothes, their rifle barrels, their belt buckles, their bayonets . . . Demirgian laughed and laughed, he couldn't help it. Foley smiled too, he understood, but another sergeant with a Korea ribbon and three battle stars noted Demirgian's frivolousness and only snarled. "Watch and see!" he said, meaning Demirgian, meaning Vietnam. "He's the one who'll be dead in one week, watch and see!"

Take ten. In its inimitable fashion, M company rose for a ten-minute rest, a sergeant shouting *"On your feet"* and M assuming an upright attitude with a heart-stopping roar of *"On guard!"* And then, with a shout from the depths of its soul it bolted from Foley's cold shack to warm itself in the great outdoors by seizing up Acropolis pieces of crusted snow and bashing them on one another's howling heads, five hundred eyebrows turning white, ice water trickling down two hundred and fifty necks, the apoplectic sergeants running from one to another Siberian skirmish to try to end hostilities which they considered unbecoming to men in uniform, one of these spoilsports nearly swallowing Demirgian's nose in his contiguous fury. *"Soldier, wasn't that you lifting a snowball?"*

"No, sergeant," Demirgian answered honestly—a ball it wasn't.

"Well maybe I'm stupid, maybe I'm just stupid, soldier," actually there was no maybe about it. *"Do you really think I'm stupid?"*

"No, sergeant," Demirgian answered tactfully.

"All right," the sergeant said, hurrying off to another snow-slab fight with the satisfaction of having Demirgian's guarantee that he wasn't actually stupid. By early evening the snow in this windblown

simulated artillery, throwing his little cherry bombs to M's left and right. One hour ahead of M the enemy waited, all of its brazen aggressors simulated by Private McCarthy.

Lucky Mac. As tonight's duly appointed foe he had built himself a fire, he had seated himself on a log while he stoically bided his time until he would be annihilated, high and dry he had given himself to that rarest of GI moments: time to think, time to try to reconstitute his past, present, and future, time to examine a life whose humble ingredients he had given the Army on a silver platter, only to have it dropped in a garbage bin in one great succotash splash. McCarthy had enlisted voluntarily: enlisted would mean his getting his choice of Army careers: A CHOICE NOT A CHANCE, the Army's red, white, and blue recruiting poster had catchily phrased it. McCarthy's shrewd choice had been to sign up for three idyllic years in the military police, a corps of boys whose leisurely promenades by foot and by Chevrolet from one to another downtown tavern held out a promise of life expectancy that the infantry didn't. Simple survival was no mean consideration to this civilian, an American with fifty attractive years of life and limb ahead and a genuine reluctance to suffer the loss of either. But what was McCarthy's undoing was that the Army's recruiting poster had chosen a sort of WPA monumental style to illustrate the soldier's life, it hadn't used the hon-

est realism of Jackson Pollock and McCarthy's
crafty plans had started to go agley from his very
first day of the GI jive. Scarcely had the necessary
papers been signed and sealed, raise your right
hand, shake, than it seemed to the Army's newest
military policeman-designate to be about ten seconds before his sweater with its he-man leather elbow patches, his shirt, his charcoal-gray summer
slacks, had been pulled from his mortified body, his
hair had been shaved from his muddled head, his
blood itself had been modified with Army additives,
jab—jab—jab. A pair of tin license plates was chained
to McCarthy's captive neck and everywhere that he
walked he clinked, as though he might need a valve
job. *Right face—left face—Simon says about face*—Mc-
Carthy was marched in most of the directions known
to science all that chaotic afternoon, *go back you
didn't say may I,* and at sundown he was dressed in a
clown's costume of white and orange spiral stripes,
the better to help other vertiginous soldiers to cross
the company street. His reign as the peppermint-
stick fairy not having ended till 1, at 3 he was
shaken awake to dress in his itchy fatigues and
*come-and-get-your-beans-boys, come-and-get-your-
beans,* and serve soldiers scrambled eggs, and *you've-
got-to-get-up, you've-got-to-get-up,* it was dawn of his
second day in the Army. Now fall outside! Forward
march! Dive for the oyster! Dig for the clam! Tossed
in a blanket, turned like a top, 8 in the morning
found him in a state of mind distortion that the federal laws themselves say a man mustn't attempt except under a doctor's care. A yellow pencil lay in
McCarthy's boneless hand. His rickety elbows sat on
a wooden desk. At this sudden instant between his
birth and death our poor catatonic learned to his
mortal horror that he would endure a series of fifteen
written tests, nine hundred diversified questions
that all united into the mightiest question of all, *(a)*

him into consciousness again, 6 . . . 7 . . . 8 . . . 9 . . . 10. . . . Anatomy and naughty words kept grinning at him from his test paper's circumjacencies, the scratches of past prisoners of this Chillon, GO NAVY and FUCK UNCLE SAM, a last delirious stab at reality, 11 . . . 12 . . . ɛı . . . 14 . . . ɕı . . . . The questions themselves weren't any to help him recover his senses, 16 . . . ıʃ' . . . 18 . . . ıθ' . . . 20. . . . Many were so outwardly bland that he couldn't believe they didn't conceal some Sphinxical trick, *a dog is a kind of (a) bird, (b) flower, (c) stone, (d) animal.* Some of the Army's questions were of college caliber, others were so sickly introspective that the very act of thinking about them encouraged psychosis, *which of these describes you better, (a) generous, (b) kind.* There was a Morse code listening test, one hundred and fifty squeaky sets of *dit*s and *dah*s prefaced by two hundred and seventy *dah*s and *dit*s to practice upon, and there was a driver's test whose two hundred and forty weirdo questions needed no ignition key to answer, ooooCOCOoooOCOOO, *how many* C's *are there?* Warm little butterballs, McCarthy's eyes couldn't see his driver's test as anything but a totally O-less C-less rod of gray. And horror of horrors, whenever he scratched his bewildered head in the usual adjuratory gesture of eking out answers— *where did it go?* his head wasn't his, his noodle had been supplanted by *(a) a coconut, (b) a canteloupe, (c) a volleyball, or (d) somebody else's—somebody bald* *and awful.* In—out—in—out—the warehouse room he was writing in seemed to be breathing, its four wooden walls were a paper bag on McCarthy's suffering head. His cerebrum's convolutions curled onto one another tighter, his blood drained into his spinal cord as water would from a wringed-out mop, his line of thought took a series of wild encephalographic angles, *who would the Army want in its military police, (a) generous, (b) kind, who would the Army send to Vietnam, (a) generous, (b) kind, how can I think without my head, give— me— back— my golden head!* The hole in the ceiling shrieking, *"Stop,"* his pencil darting away like a dragonfly, his answer sheet like a paper airplane, the score on his driver's test an 84, the maximum 140, a 90 the minimum for military police, the moving finger now having writ moved on—the Army now trundled his shattered soul to the infantry, to basic training to infantry training in M. At M, McCarthy wasn't alone in his disenchantment. Sullivan had once had a speeding ticket—infantry. Prochaska was only eighteen—infantry. In spite of the poster promises, M could field a squad or two of wistful rejects from the military police who had volunteered for the Army without being shown the fine print under the words, A CHOICE NOT A CHANCE.

And so this snowy evening, contingency had arranged for Mac to sit in the orange glow of his campfire, an uncommitted colloid in a state of suspension between before and after, life and death—a Rodin thinker in a museum closed for the night. Twenty-one years old, he had that doughy sort of Irish face whose nose and lips appear to be pressed on a windowpane, the eyes of this oatmeal cookie at times two little raisins of fear, at other times two empty surfaces of certainty: and this glowing night it was certainty. Tonight this pensive soldier saw nothing but a little orange sphere of reassurance, beyond

South Vietnam. Saturday would be his wedding day in Islip, Long Island. So far so good: *I do.* A wife entitling him to another $95.20 a month, on Monday the sergeants would send him to personnel to fill in mimeographed forms: and while he was there he would arrange that the cuckoo "oooocococoooo-cooo"s of the driver's test be administered to him again during his waking hours. The natural order of things being to go to Georgia's training center for military police, he figured that he could pay for his and his bride's apartment by selling his Ford for $500. The left rear window he would keep for himself, he wanted to hang it and its seventeen red, orange, and yellow decals that he had earned in drag racing over his Georgia fireplace. Removing that one rear window wouldn't be any great matter. With his Phillips screwdriver he would loosen the four easy Phillips screws and—

Ta-ta-ta-ta-ta-ta-ta! Out of the black came the first of Foley's howling patrols, firing from its striding hips and throwing its noisy Fourth of July grenades, its rifles filling the night with a swarm of little campfire colors, its battle cries of *aargh* tearing the night to shreds. Obediently, McCarthy fell to the crunchy snow and simulated having died, his real prospects in life as bright and benign as a trip on a child's tricycle.

Saturday he went to Islip and married a girl named Marilyn. After the civil ceremony they returned to her living room to look at the Hofstra game on channel eleven, late in the last period McCarthy asking the girl of his cautious dreams, "Where'll we eat tonight?"

"I don't know, where'll we eat?" Marilyn asked.

"I don't know, where'll we eat?"

"I don't know, you've got the car keys."

The father of this bride, sitting in his undershirt in a Barcalounger, drinking a Bud, and dropping his cigarette ashes into a tray whose crockery rose in the center like a silver epergne to imitate the shapes of a bowling ball and a bowling pin—Marilyn's father was a Michelin of table tips, "Well, how about Captain Marty's?" "How about Captain Bill's?" Marilyn had promised this member of the wedding to finish her high school if he would give his grumpy consent.

"Well, where'll we go to eat?" Marilyn asked.

"I guess we'll go to Captain Bill's," her husband answered.

But he would go to Vietnam—or so rumor had it. Talk of that remote Martian area proliferated now in M's last week of training, and rumors became as prevalent as sugar maple seeds in spring—no, they seemed to generate spontaneously, phrases, names, and numbers, the particles of old forgotten sentences, seemed to sigh through the barracks windows and gravitate together, to gather to a greatness like the ooze of oil crushed, to kiss and coalesce like window rime, and *listen . . . listen . . . listen in the seashell . . .* there would be another rumor, born to grow corpulent on M's wistful hopes and restless fears. One of these free-floating messages went, M was being posted to Vietnam *in toto,* all its diverse sergeants included. At other times the wind whispered to M's subtle ears: Germany, M was being sent

low Army biographical record, his civil marriage certificate with its pretty little verse from *Hiawatha*, his mimeographed $95.20 form, his Army enlistment contract with its bittersweet promise of *military police*, two special beckoning words like a Maltese cross on a treasure map, *come to me . . . come to me . . .* going to personnel, McCarthy had turned the color of library paste when the clerk assured him secretly that one hundred and forty-four *(sic)* of M's unwitting casuals were on Vietnam orders, McCarthy among them. But then the blabbermouthed clerk did in one half minute what M's soft-hearted first sergeant had still not accomplished in half a week, he discovered that he had good—well: *miraculous*—news for Private McCarthy. Frowning with black-browed intensity at this unwilling infantryman's yellow case history record, he announced that the score on McCarthy's fatal driver's test wasn't an 84 at all, rather it was a big black clerical splat that a man of compassion could just as readily believe was a 94—a 94, a passing mark for the military police! The clerk having promised to bring this serious error to the assistant adjutant's attention, McCarthy walked out of personnel and walked back to M so airily that one would have scarcely guessed he was wearing galoshes.

Interestingly, it lay within M's powers on these last rumor-ridden days to exempt itself from Vietnam duty. Any extremely reluctant soldier could do this through the Machiavellian trick of flunking the finals, another of those all-inclusive *(a) (b) (c) (d)* and *(true) (false)* affairs that the Army would administer on Thursday. Nor would the Army's questions be so ridiculously puerile that a boy would be ashamed to answer wrong, *on a night patrol animal sounds or bird sounds should be used for control (true) (false)*, not every sap in America would know it was false. But though a boy could purposely "bolo" his written test or froth at the mouth and faint on his physical test, he would just be surrendering to a fate abominably worse than a year in the steaming jungles: two more months of infantry training at M, and every boy in M could be trusted to have on his thinking cap on Thursday. The evening before, M had a cram session in its cellarlike barracks and it was SRO, Demirgian, of course, absenting himself for a frothy beer and another one or two squads unconcernedly awol: and Mallory, a big Negro sergeant with a build that was uninterrupted muscle from his head to his very dense toes, now opened the class by saying, "Gentlemens," with a voice out of *Old Man River*— "Gentlemens, if you aren't here tonight, shame on you—shame on you."

There is truth to the soldiers' saying, the Army is a device built by geniuses to be driven by— idiots is too strong a word, men of average intelligence is fairer. Tonight's teacher Mallory was no great brains and Mallory would never deny it, for this embarrassing oversight a sense of impartiality finds that the Lord himself must be gently blamed. And yet, Mallory had become a sergeant of many shining

...ing, Mallory's taste wasn't educated: give him a vase of daisies and Mallory's sense of aesthetics would be Egyptian, he promptly would put it in the geometric center of the coffee table. Mallory was Demirgian's nemesis, the haircut sergeant, the purist for whose sensibilities all of M's craniums had to be austere as the pyramids, its footlockers parallel as the pedestals of Karnak. Given his classical way, the toilet articles in those ever-loving footlockers wouldn't just correspond but coincide, the toothpaste would be Pepsodent everywhere, the bristles would sit in brushes of harmonizing green—when Mallory was a private all of his barracks had to buy homogeneously, those were the days! And tonight when Mallory began his cram class his sense of monolithic order put first things first. His tuba voice roared out to M, "Seats!" "On your feet!" "Seats!" "On your feet!" "Seats!" "On your feet!" "Seats!" "On your feet!" "Seats!" for verse after verse until he had M seating itself with the lovely synchronization of bowling pins in one of those—*clop!*—automatic pin-setting machines.

Mallory had a second far-from-tragic flaw. He hadn't the philosopher's passion to look beneath glistering surfaces for ultimate truths, Mallory took it for granted that if a marksman's medal was centered the heart and soul beneath it were consequently squared away. Before all inspections Mallory would say to M in his *tote-dat-barge* and *lift-dat-bale* voice,

"Peoples, all of your khaki shirts. I want everyone get himself an iron and iron the left sleeve," because in the wall lockers that is the plenary sleeve, the plenipotentiary sleeve, the sleeve that the Captain or Major would see as he trotted by—the *be-all* and the *end-all* sleeve. No names, but Mallory knew of footlockers in M whose immaculate toothbrushes lay in their permanent showcase like a little Cellini necklace, totally untouched by human teeth. Far from being peeved at a boy whose secret workaday toothbrush might be the shape of a poodle's tail or the color of kelp, Mallory was pleased with the boy's expensive initiative. As for tomorrow's finals, from Mallory's somewhat simple point of view a soldier who scored 150 out of 150 would be *ipso facto* a one-hundred percent qualified soldier—and so to Mallory's conscience there was nothing amiss or immoral in the course of study that he had prepared for tonight. Having gotten M to seat itself with the accuracy of the Rockettes, Mallory meant to do nothing less astonishing than to reveal all of Thursday's answers. All of the Army's questions—all of the Army's answers.

Now, it wasn't that Mallory had pilfered the tests from the dean's office or anything like it—no. Mallory had simply become aware as M after M went through training that the Army's questions had scarcely changed from one to another cycle, and showing initiative he had kept copies of these hoary questions: Mallory had a little list, and M cocked its collective ear as its enterprising sergeant began to recite it tonight. "Gentlemens," he said in his marvelous voice, alone of M's sergeants he understood that his *a*'s and *o*'s should not just start in his stomach but leave it as well, "Gentlemens, number one. Prior to departure from the assembly area, a patrol should *(a)* write a letter home, *(b)* rehearse, *(c)* study the code of conduct, *(d)* all of the above."

. . . . cigarettes Mallory
bent the passing minutes back on themselves and
started through his questions a second time, the
Army's system of pedagogy being the same as Madi-
son Avenue's, perpetual repetition repetition. This
time when Mallory asked what a patrol should do at
H-hour minus, M all shouted back, "Rehearse!" The
third time, Mallory hadn't even advanced the first of
his four tactical options before he was interrupted by
a mighty synchronous roar, "Rehearse!" and Mallory gave M his golden smile, Mallory's great heart
was jubilant, Mallory knew. M was becoming sensi-
tized to what a patrol must do prior to its departure
from the assembly area—it must rehearse. But by
his fourth go-around, Mallory's ritual question
seemed to be getting soggy at its edges like a spoiled
peach, and a note of irritation seemed to have pene-
trated M's "Rehearse." By the fifth time, the wheel
of receptivity had turned full circle and M's familiar
reply was a shapeless murmur, ". . . Rehearse." The
hour was getting on towards 10 o'clock, the clock itself was sagging at its 4-5-6-7-8's like one of Dali's
languishing watches, paint was peeling from its
hour hand and settling to the barracks floor like
sootfall. M had been awake since 4 o'clock.

Mallory wasn't deaf: he recognized that he was
now losing his audience. With the roar of a Nebu-
chadnezzar ordering, "On your knees," Mallory
called out, "On your feet!" and M slowly pushed itself

to a hominid posture while it stated with no real sparkle, "On guard."

"Seats!" and "Blue bolts," and as Mallory continued into his sixth little minuet his wits could be confident that M's old arteries were again carrying oxygen to its memory cells.

But his system worked. Thursday after a lunch of master menu, the butterscotch pie deleted and butterscotch pudding in its crispy stead, there in its chilly messhall practically all of M company passed its 1 . . . 2 . . . 3 . . . 4 . . . finals and qualified itself to wage war in Asia or to loll around in Europe in the coming year, a couple of acting sergeants scoring 147 out of 150 and M company's average well up in the 100's.

Demirgian got 108. Thus, by Mallory's arithmetic Demirgian's heart was pumping seventy-two percent fighting blood—a questionable correlation. Not all of the *(a) (b) (c) (d)* and *(true) (false)* questions could be said to have measured M's sagacity or even its common sense. Whoever had written them suffered from that common misconception, the nomenclatural fallacy, the belief that any phenomenon's name is all ye need to know on this Barry and Enright earth, the mental aberration of American ladies in art museums—ladies who pause to say *"Cezanne!"* and triumphantly go to the next pretty $64,000 question. Most of the Army's time-honored questions, Mallory's questions, were of this onomastic sort, *three types of combat patrol are (a) area, ambush, security, (b) area, security, economy of forces, (c) route, security, ambush, (d) ambush, contact, economy of forces,* the imagination reels to think of the scholarly foxhole where this intelligence would be of much military use. Indeed, the only boy at M with a past record of courage and competence under fire was a wiry private who finished his pencil-and-paper finals in fifteen minutes and scored 144, and rolling his eyes

ᴜ..ᴜ, ooon as you raise it by then they're
on top of you with bayonets. Same with the karate
stuff. I listen to that sergeant he tells me about
karate, he says to stand and do *this,* do *that* do *this,*
do *that,*" as Mason kept crooking himself into the ex-
otic postures that are recommended by the Army's
karate sergeants and adopted by the figures on
friezes on Hindu temples, "all of that karate jive.
Forget it—I'm sent to Vietnam, I'm taking in you
know what? A razor. You don't believe me? A
straight-edge razor and a towel. A towel, I wrap it
around my wrist and maybe you scratch me—I promise you won't hurt me. A razor I killed you thirty seconds ago!"

(True) (false)—a rhetorical question. Mason had
cocked his whole body into a question mark and
every muscle in it was crying *isn't it true?* Mason had
learned about arms and the juvenile man in the
fields of Harlem, Mason was born and brought up on
100th street. *Three ways to camouflage yourself are*
. . . Mason didn't need to know, already he was
blacker than an ironwood tree, and evenings when
he had hidden in doorways the Law had walked as
close as— *that,* without seeing him. *Three types of ambushes are* . . . Mason knew two or three hundred, as
early as ten years old he had sergeanted one. It was
summer then, on the parapets of Harlem's tene-
ments he had arrayed his weapons: bottles and
bricks, some of the Coke bottles full of what little

gasoline his ambush patrol had had the money to buy. On the sidewalk below, five of Mason's brave little friends had acted as decoys by playing catch, and when the Enchanters kept their bloodthirsty promise and swooped onto Mason's peace-loving street an hour after sunset—and three hundred strong—the decoys had skipped into alleys, and Mason's youthful patrol had thrown down garbage cans at either end of the block and panicked the Enchanters into the center. And then Mason's beardless army had double-timed it along the rooftops, pushing the rest of its tonnage onto the Enchanters' deserving heads. When he was twice that age, Mason of M company once had to sit through a chalk talk on the topic of horseshoe ambushes, and rolling his world-weary eyes to the heavens he had whispered, "Big deal. So now they've got a name for it."

At ten Mason had organized a Harlem street gang and become its president: its captain. Let the words *juvenile delinquent* lie, Mason had started as just the opposite. He had become aware that his elementary education was being disrupted by a series of recurrent headaches, and attributing this to the baseball bats the Enchanters would use on this susceptible part of his skeleton whenever he walked to his grade school he had simply asked six of his abecedarian friends to accompany him mornings and afternoons: *everyone cheese it, a Harlem gang!* The rest of his formative years, Mason had withstood the onslaught of guns, of switchblade knives and straight-edge razors, of Harlem's sticks and stones, and Mason had learned to reply in kind. Having come of age in America in the course of a patriotic war, Mason had volunteered for the Army: a self-assured young man, he now hoped to go to the continent where he could turn his hard-gotten talents to profit. "For once, I'd like to cut someone's throat and be paid for it," Ma-

calms of time's continuum, the Past had been struck like a carnival tent at summer's end, the Future hadn't been raised yet, all of M's clocks were out being wound. M was in touch with the absolute tonight—and as whenever sophomores and philosophy meet, the dialogues were all ambitious, temerarious, erratic, paralogical, and ultimately incoherent. Life and death and other ontological thoughts that M had never before or after had on its busy minds went fluttering through its conversations like spooky Cecropia moths, and Tennessee was saying to Mason, "That ain't no reason to go to Vietnam."

"Oh, that ain't no reason? Then answer me, give me a reason!" Mason replied as he coiled himself in his *(true) (false)* posture, his eyes as bright as tensor lamps.

"All right then, a reason. Strategically—"

"Uh-uh! I don't care about stragetic—stratetic—*ffft!*" and Mason just whistled impotently, his *t*'s and *g*'s getting stuck in his body's energetic knots.

"Strategically most of the people live in the North," the Tennessee soldier earnestly said, his scraggy little legs protected by white woolen underwear, his grasp of economic geography tightened by a very persuasive new article in *Reader's Digest.* To sanity's chagrin, his arguments would not be seen through a microscope but through a kaleidoscope—when the earnest conversation of soldiers or sophomores takes a new turn it *swerves.*

"Then answer me this," Mason was interrupting him. "Why do the most people live in the North? Why?"

"Aww, what do you mean why? How can I explain why? Most of the people live in the North because that's where the biggest concentration of population is."

"All right, answer me this. Communism so detestable why don't the most people live in the South?"

"Because of America stopping them, let me finish! In the Delta, all of the rice occurs in the Delta, also all of the water. America is trying to stop all that large population in the North from getting to the rice and water, that is the reason our being in South Vietnam. Because as soon as they've also got Malaya the shipping lanes to Japan—"

"Oh man. Oh man. Oh man. I'm sorry, but you're *dead!*" and Mason wasn't just jiving the Tennessee global strategist, Mason believed it, manifest destiny, the Spanish succession, get in a fight for those listless ideals or for Japanese shipping lanes and you're— *dead,* never in Mason's asphalt jungles had a boy survived on such delicate cotton candy. "Oh man, you're going to be in that slimy foxhole, you've got a buddy his throat is split and there's blood coming out, and you're going to *shriek*— and jump outside and step on a mine, *you're dead.*" Mason could see the tragedy clearly, to his pitying eyes the Tennessee soldier lay on the black rubber sheet even now, he ought to be buried before he could decompose.

"And you're? You're going to what?"

"A dead man in my foxhole I'm going to live, I promise you," Mason replied. "I'm going to sit there till my relief, I'm going to say good morning, this is your field of fire, that's a guy in your foxhole got himself killed, out over there's a ditch go and bury him, I'm going to say goodbye, I'm going back to my tent and I'm ....

*I'm coming out alive, I promise—promise—*the sacred words that Mason's invincible spirit gave to his vulnerable flesh: Mason's, and each and every soldier's in M,

It happened that at this Thursday evening bull session two religious soldiers name of Smith had been sitting along the gray barracks wall and listening quietly, one of these Smith soldiers white, the other of them a Negro. One of them was Smith the visionary, the Penseroso who might or might not be serving God's will while dutifully serving the Army's and praying that God take the rap. The other Smith was a Harlem boy, a Saturday night gang fighter and a Sunday Christian, no contradiction there: a boy born in Harlem may reasonably come to believe he needs heaven's help or the help of ten or a dozen muscular friends whenever heaven's is not forthcoming. *I'm coming out of Vietnam alive.* . . . It was Mason's mystical faith in his being the object of God's special grace that got these two pious Smiths to speak their minds, the Negro saying to the white one, "Daddy, now you're a preacher, right? You remember where Mason got taught that? You recollect the ninety-first psalm?"

"Um . . . ," Smith the white preacher replied. He believed that as God's chosen messenger *(perhaps)* it was morally incumbent upon him to carry the ninety-first psalm on his tongue tip at all occasions. "Um . . . the ninety-first psalm . . . the ninety-first. . . ."

"Go get a Bible, daddy," and Smith the white falterer hurried to his footlocker to bring God's word out of its authorized ark.

"Um . . . ," Smith said, coming back to the area, "Kings . . . ," sitting and turning the Bible's whispering pages, "Job . . . ought to be hereabouts . . . here, the ninety-first psalm. . . ."

"Verse number five, daddy. Check it out."

"Yes . . . yes, of course . . . ," Smith continued, and then by the flame of Mason's cigarette lighter, the barracks light being dim, he started to read the Bible aloud. *"Thou shalt not be afraid,"* Smith began—*"thou shalt not be afraid for the terror by night; nor for the arrow that flieth by day; nor for the pestilence that walketh in darkness; nor for the destruction that wasteth at noonday."*

"Stand by, daddy. It's coming."

"A thousand shall fall," Smith continued—*"a thousand shall fall at thy side, and ten thousand at thy right hand; but it shall not come nigh thee."*

"Daddy, it shall not come nigh! So chalk that up! That's on the wall!" Smith the Negro soldier said. In other words: because of God's particular concern in his survival or some special inextinguishability of spirit or—well, simply because—whatever mayhem the future was to wreak upon the rest of M, the word of God promised it couldn't happen to Smith: Smith the Negro street fighter really believed it. Smith the white preacher also believed it. Demirgian, whose family name was Smith (Smith in Armenian), believed it, every boy in M believed it, therefore it couldn't be true.

...........g about the barracks that was—
low, it was like a bare light bulb at the bottom of a
mine shaft, one in which big brown caterpillars slept
on the walls. Of course it was black outside. A transistor radio that had distantly played rock-and-roll
through the night now shouted "Go! Go! Go!" to
some unimaginable audience, and an announcer
chortled, "It's cold and windy and by *George!* I'm
going to tell you, it's going to be cold all day—the
high in the twenties!" Someone in M said "Damn"
and others muttered things about two sorts of
'uckers from under brown blankets that still hadn't
moved. Wherever that radio station was, it wasn't on
M's planet, where time ran at a fraction of that
speed. The news was that Johnson had met his se-
nior advisors again amid indications that he would
do blah-blah-blah, something about Vietnam.

For breakfast M ate a master menu, no food deleted or substituted, and then it shuffled outside for a
6 o'clock flag ceremony, forming its shadowy ranks
on the snow. In front of M stood Doherty, its first sergeant, his doldrums not quite driven away by two
black coffees that he had drunk beneath the messhall's peeling fresco of Roman charioteers while
he gloomily ran a thumbnail down a manila envelope and muttered to himself, "Bad day at Black Rock
. . . Bad day at Black Rock." Now a bugle sounded,
issuing from a drab signal corps MX-39A/TIQ-2 record
player at the adjutant's office a half mile away. M sa-

luted. Somewhere in the night an American flag was rising, but M saw only its desolate barracks lights and above them in the south the cold constellations of Sagittarius, Scorpio, and Libra. When the music ended, Doherty dropped his salute and spinning around to the company said, "At ease! The following enlisted personnel have received orders for Vietnam—when I call your name answer and fall out to the dayroom. Arrington!" There was silence. *"Arrington!"*

"He's on KP," said a voice, and Doherty continued hastily down his typewritten list.

Thus did M company come to apprehend its destiny. Later that day it would have theories why this or that soldier had or hadn't been chosen, phrases like *shuffle the cards, names in a hat, darts on a dartboard,* and *you-you-you* would be heard through the noisy barracks, but never would M guess that the moving finger had been its own: for Swizzlestick's mimeographed forms had long before been papered over in its memory by a dozen others. One shrewd theory that day would owe to a Florida boy, an alligator trapper name of Newman who just couldn't reconcile himself to a random universe. Observing that he himself, Williams of Florida, Morton of Texas, and Yoshioka of California were on Vietnam orders, he would reason that the Army sent soldiers there from the southern tier of states, experienced boys who would acclimate to the heat—a plausible hypothesis that would have several adherents. Of course it was only coincidence, Newman had asked for Japan and Williams had been given a bum deal: he was near the bottom of the green IBM deck, and Pulver, smoking his corncob pipe and reaching the card of that gentle Negro periscope operator, had realized he hadn't enough places left in Europe for every soldier who wanted one. At last letting his fingers obey the haphazard electrical impulses from his

speaking quietly. His handkerchief had gotten that way after his nose began bleeding after he started crying after he stopped laughing, the first of his three violent reactions to the news he now gave to Jirier: "I've got orders to Vietnam." His lady-killing friend Sullivan, who still dreamt he would go to the Caribbean and be dating girls in yellow bikinis, fell out to the clamorous dayroom to learn if Doherty's cry of "Sullivan!" meant him or M's one other Sullivan.

"Which one is RA1146 . . . ," Doherty began.

"Here, sergeant," Sullivan said.

"All right, the other Sullivan may leave," and Sullivan thought, *what the hell—?* looking hurt, falling back on the ice-cream vending machine. Bigalow, who wanted to go to Vietnam but couldn't notify the Pentagon because he was washing pans—Bigalow was wreathed in smiles, but then he was always smiles, he looked like one of those faces on porcelain Bavarian beer mugs that smile and smile self-satisfiedly whether a mug is full or empty. Not finding anything by Bigalow's name but an X meaning no known preference, Pulver had assigned him to Vietnam. Assigned to Vietnam, McCarthy, the married man, at once turned the color of egg-drop soup and fled across the snow to the assistant adjutant's to prove to him that the enigmatic splat on his Army biographical record wasn't an 84 but a 94 instead. Nobody's fool, the assistant adjutant said that Mc-

Carthy had *nerve* to go splattering ink on his Army record, he ought to be court-martialed, scram. Smith, the unstrung puppet of God's departed will, might or mightn't go to Vietnam in God's good time but first he would go to officer candidate school to become a second lieutenant. "I'm going to Vietnam and would you believe it? I'm happy," Hofelder, the bony Philadelphia boy who didn't think much of periscopes, was saying to guys, little guessing that one hour later personnel was to have a cable from Pulver reassigning him to Fort Lewis, Washington. Russo, the Lochinvar who joined when he was sixteen, stood in the noisy dayroom and made quick soldierly stabs and butt strokes with a mimical bayonet: he was going to Vietnam gleefully, though he wasn't even of age to be in the Army. *We're all in it together*—M was happy about that, and there was hearty shaking of hands, slapping of backs, as M watched the dayroom filling with the same sea of familiar faces that had blotted out the rest of the universe, literally! except in the lonely toilet and shower stalls, for eight weeks, and which would be snugly around it in the year to come. Most boys in M were happy to go where they'd have friends; where the sergeants wouldn't order them around and it wouldn't snow—honored, if a little surprised, that America had found them equal to the manly task of defending it.

Someone said, "What's the matter with Chaska?" Since everyone in M wore his family name stenciled over his shirt pocket, naturally he was known by some pleasant diminutive of it—Smitty, Willy, Sully, Demirge, Mac for McCarthy, Yoyo for Yoshioka, or Chaska for Prochaska, the boy who believed in hamburgers, patriotic songs, and Vietnam, who now stood leaning across the upper deck of his bunk, sobbing, his shoulders making his iron bedstead rattle, his voice choking on the words, "This is too much. My nerves . . . my nerves are gone," and "This is the

Swizzlestick's mimeographed form—Swizzlestick, knowing that Sweden was neutral with no American troops there, ~~had changed it to Europe,~~ and Pulver had assigned him to Germany. No—Prochaska was at this extremity because of a chain of circumstances starting at the very soldier who asked, "What's the matter with Chaska?" Some nights before, ironing his Army greens, that careless fellow had burned Prochaska's hand with the iron, causing a raw wound. Naturally enough, Prochaska didn't want to put this painful hand in a tub of hot water frothing with GI lye-soap when he was assigned to do KP in K company's kitchen on this momentous Friday morning. It happened, though, that K's was the very kitchen that the General had given his monthly award to, a wooden plaque with a bronze shield with a quasi-heraldic device on it, a chef's-cap imposed on a stirring spoon dexter on three saucepans—a plaque that K's burly mess sergeant anxiously wished to retain in its place of honor over the vegetable steamers, his name was Sergeant Soda. So when Prochaska, told to plunge his wounded member into the pots and pans in that alkaline vat, politely had to demur, is everyone still with us, Soda was annoyed that a rival company had jeopardized his preeminence by sending him KPs who were half-crippled, and Soda's culinary staff took its revenge by riding on Prochaska mercilessly, yelling at him, "Hurry up! Faster! Let's go! Let's get on with it," as he scrubbed the little lines of cement between the glazed tiles on Soda's floor. Unable to take it and fleeing to M's friendly sanctuary, Prochaska now leaned on his bunk in tears, trying to collect himself. He moaned, "I used to like KP, it was lots of fun. But now . . . *I wish I were going to Vietnam*, just so I could get out of this!"

As indeed he would have. Because—with the upper echelons approving—all the men assigned to Vietnam were to get their weekend passes that very afternoon, this had been Doherty's good news. He broke it to M's expeditionary force when it had gathered in the fluorescent dayroom. He said, at 8 o'clock that morning they'd have their communism class, at 9 they'd have a long review of Army drill, the left-face right-face business, the last lesson of infantry training, at 12 they'd be back to eat master menu, and when the gray barracks were in apple-pie order they would have— passes, they would have Friday as well as Saturday night to be with their families before going off to war, though it meant missing the Colonel's own inspection. Sunday they'd—Doherty said sternly that *they'd be back by Sunday midnight*, Monday to Wednesday they'd fill in mimeographed forms, get their underwear dyed forest green, Thursday they'd graduate, Friday they'd go to Vietnam. "Now! We had to go as high as Brigadier General Ekman," Doherty said. "Men, you can show your appreciation for those three-day passes by getting back on Sunday night!"

"Yes, sergeant!" M replied—the passes were all it thought about.

"You aren't back you *will* be court-martialed. Men," Doherty's voice now dropping like a phonograph record when the plug is pulled, "this isn't just being awol. This is called missing a movement. Men," dropping and dropping, "I think it holds something like six years and a dishonorable dis-

Men— it was the Captain speaking, "Men, they're making a guinea pig of my company. You guys can be selfish and not come back on Sunday or come back too pooped to pop. Then you'll upset the applecart, they'll never give us three-day passes again!"

"Remember what's coming up behind you!" Doherty put in. "Fifteen thousand guys and you'll be meeting them all through life. Fifteen thousand guys who won't be able to say bye-bye if you're not back on Sunday!" ·

"You've got my ass hanging on a lamppost," the Captain cried. *"You can lower me down or leave me there! So—ARE YOU GUYS COMING BACK ON SUNDAY?"*

"Yes . . . *sir!"* M shouted back.

"All right. I'll be waiting for you," the Captain concluded.

And then M went to its communism class, and then it went out to practice marching as Mallory sang it the cadence: Mallory, the voice of thunder! The sergeant's breath made steam as he called into the morning air, *"Lift your head and hold it high! Mighty Mike is passing by! Am . . . I right or wrong?"*

"You're right!" M shouted back as its right feet put a drumbeat in, a *right* on the snow-covered ground.

"Delayed cadence! Mike cadence! Company cadence! Count!" Mallory now sang out.

And his company answered, "*M . . . I . . . K . . . E! . . . M . . . I . . . K . . . E! Migh . . . ty Mike! Migh . . . ty Mike! Fight fight FIGHT!*" as little wisps of windblown snow curled around its marching feet.

Mighty Mike Is
Passing By!

has a loved one in his arms—no. Sullivan's girl was in Stowe doing parallel turns, and Sullivan sat reconciledly on a stool in his mother's yellow kitchen murmuring "Commonwealth 6-1234" and "Adams 2-2000" into an imaginary telephone. His giggling youngest sister, her teeth glittering happily, her fingers scribbling marks on a set of stiff IBM cards, was crying to Sullivan, *"Ooh . . . faster,"* practicing to be a telephone operator. Williams's girl was in Florida lovelorn, a can of Williams's favorite creamed corn in her Frigidaire, the Army's finance office having put the two asunder. Something was wrong at finance, it hadn't paid Williams for months, on Saturday he couldn't leave camp, he went to the movies with California's lonely Yoshioka: *Beachball,* the movie's name. Bigalow met a girl at a YMCA dance and *touché,* Bigalow kissed her good-night, his greenwood tree the portico to her boarding house, his feet turning numb in the snow, his home was in Oregon and $141 away. But in Greenwich Village that winter's evening in the if-I-had-a-hammer-loud pad of four cuckoo defrocked monks, one soldier who really *swung* was a PFC whose relevance is that he worked 8 to 5 at the finance office, managing M's pay. M's long history of indigence shouldn't be laid to this happy PFC, though. No beatnik himself, he was devoted to his dusty little adding machine except—alas, the servant of two sergeants, he was a soldier first, a pay clerk second. Friday at camp he had pulled KP, Saturday he had watched a movie on guerilla warfare: no exaggeration, the tenth time. Sunday the dingy finance office wouldn't be open, Monday he would have the snow-shoveling detail, Tuesday morning all systems go! the PFC could work on M's old musty pay records, his rain-cloud-colored fluorescent lights flickering till after midnight, his adding machine making its lonely metallic sounds, but Wednesday he would have the laundry detail, Thursday he would see more movies, Friday he— but Friday, M would go to Vietnam. This had been the PFC's predicament for many months.

With a real physical telephone, Sullivan called up his schussing girl friend's good friend, Debbie, and asked her to the Saturday night movies, he couldn't go parking with her, in conscience. Across town in his family's crazily gabled house, Demirgian sat with his schoolmates as they played whist at a round oaken table—*whist!* Once it was hula hoops, the Beatles, now in Massachusetts the teenagers were playing knock-whist and eating knackwurst as they talked of civilian times. "Remember the assistant principal—Mr. Silvia? Saliva we called him? Mr. Spit? Remember . . . ," Demirgian was saying, playing a club, wearing a soft yellow jersey.

"What do you learn in the Army?" a friend of his interrupted, winning the trick, raking the cards in, *clack!*

"How to catch monkeys," Demirgian answered, and as their game of whist hung in sudden abeyance he explained to his awed cronies how to survive in the jungle on monkey meat. Hollow out a coconut, Demirgian said, quoting a class on the basics of Robinson Crusoeism. Tie it to something, put in a chunk of coconut white, and hide, Demirgian continued. "Well—so the dumb monkey, when he puts in his hand thinking *gee, I got me a nice piece of coconut,* the dumbbell can't pull it out again because of

cowboy rode across Marlboro country to the accompaniment of unauthentic Western music. *Nya-a-a-a*, Armenian woodwinds, music to belly dance to, music to charm snakes, for Demirgian's dark-skinned family doubled its pleasures on Saturday nights by running the TV set and the stereo concurrently while it was eating purple grapes and was drinking coffee from tiny china cups. Demirgian's mother was Greek, his father was Turkish, a rug-repair man. Demirgian himself was Armenian, there was a genealogical reason for this but as soon as one grasped it it slipped away, leaving a riddle. Demirgian was born in Jaffa; his father was in Astrakhan that day repairing shoes, his mother was a war refugee in Istanbul, obstetricians in all three cities delivered the little rascal, consulting with one another by phone. Or something—it wasn't clear. Demirgian came to America when he was ten, so young that his Eastern heritages fast deserted him, leaving just the residue of three incompatible accents—a dialectal slag, a kind of *duh-uh* in his pronunciation that to those who didn't know him sounded dopey. And leaving him a real Oriental marketplace of withered old uncles and bosomy aunts, many of these incomparables now in Demirgian's living room eating his mother's grapes on the pretext of wishing her firstborn goodbye. Speaking in Turkish, her voice rising over the come-with-me-to-the-Casbah music without becoming shrill, an aunt of Demirgian's asked the gathering, "And where will Varoujan live," Varoujan being Demirgian's first name. "In the *baraka?*" thinking of the French barracks in 1939 in Syria.

"I think not," Demirgian's mother replied, the wild pipes of Yerevan continuing *nya-a-a-a.* "In the rear there might be *baraka* but in the forward areas, I think he would live in *istihkam,*" remembering the deep Turkish trenches in 1914 at Tchanak Kale. "Yes—he would live in *istihkam* in the *bataklik,*" in trenches in the swamps, a feat of Army engineering that the aunt tried politely to conceive of for five whole seconds, chewing a pistachio nut before changing the subject.

"And what will Varoujan eat? I have read," she continued, "that in Vietnam there are no other foods besides rice and fish."

"Varoujan doesn't like fish," Demirgian's mother said. "I have explained to him that he could eat grass if the liquid in it is watery, though not if the liquid is milky."

"And what did Varoujan say?"

"Varoujan said yes, the Army had told him that. I explained that he should put these grasses in water until they are tender."

"But—!" said Demirgian's aunt. "I have read that in Vietnam there is no water that one may drink."

"Woman!" Demirgian's father put in. "You yourself say there is rice in Vietnam. It follows there must be rice fields, does it not? The fields require water—it follows there must be water in Vietnam!"

"Victoria meant drinking water," Demirgian's mother explained sweetly. "But there is water in the vines and bamboo, the Army told Varoujan that. And there are monkeys to eat, Varoujan knows how to catch them. And rabbits to eat, as well. And lizards and snakes. So it seems to me, Varoujan will have other things to eat besides rice," pausing, taking a pensive sip of Turkish coffee. "Varoujan

at 12 and Sullivan drove her there in her skinny-rib sweater, minding his manners. Meanwhile, bringing their own bottles Sullivan's friends collected at his home, but when their guest of honor walked in the front door he seemed to be shorn of spirit. It was after 12. For weeks the Army had kept Sullivan rolling like a tired jalopy with a dead battery by pushing on him relentlessly—tonight Sullivan had stopped dead. *"Hey,"* a friend of his cried when he shambled in, "they're letting you go to Vietnam? I thought we wanted to *win* this war," everyone in the living room laughing.

Sullivan answered "Mmf," sinking down in the armchair, his black raincoat on, chin on his chest, a sea of weariness surging through him like the fluids of a broken boil. From a far room he could hear *Chillerama* on a television set; Sullivan guessed that his mother was close to crying and watching it tenaciously. Strange people with no letters of introduction would come to her home taking her daughters away, tomorrow the Army would abduct her only son, leaving her with the black-and-white cat, Jerome.

"So tell us! How do the guys all feel about Vi-etnam?" a boy with a J&B asked Sullivan loudly.

". . . They'll go if they've got to."

"But they don't really want to?"

". . . No, they don't."

"Hey, are they scared about going?"

". . . Yes."

"Are *you* scared about going?"

". . . Yes."

"The little guy, is he scared also? Huh?"

". . . Yes."

"Are you two going to be together?"

". . . Yes. We're going to share a foxhole," Sullivan said wearily.

". . . Always together, until forever," Demirgian mumbled, half waking up, looking around, half falling asleep again.

"Ladies and gentlemen. Our flying time to Saigon will be approximately eighteen hours. Your attention is invited to the NO SMOKING and SEAT BELT signs. Please comply when the signs are lighted. . . ."

M company was crossing to Vietnam on Northwest airlines and it didn't like the stewardesses. One of those girls in blue incredibly couldn't get it straight between the words cereal and syrup. "Miss, may I have some *cereal*," Sullivan kept begging her, the stewardess answering, *"There,"* and pointing a firm schoolmarm's finger at Sullivan's syrup. Another of those imperfect angels said to McCarthy, *"Look— there are other people on this plane,"* when the woebegone married man applied for a modest glass of milk. Over and over the stewardesses served M its breakfast—nothing else, their protocol being that it wouldn't be lunchtime till it was noontime, an hour which never caught up with M's upholstered plane as it flew the jetstreams west. Outside of Seattle the earth became dark, it was black over the Aleutians, it was so inky black in Tokyo at some impossible hour of morning, $\sqrt{-1}$ o'clock, that all Yoshioka saw of his ancestral home was a hundred blue run-

, McCarthy said to himself once he was
back in his blue reclining seat, envisioning a self-
restrained letter to the officers of Northwest airlines
and visiting all of his plaintive resentments on their
accessible heads. *Dear sirs, I am a private in the US
army and I had the pleasure to fly on one of your char-
tered planes to Vietnam.* Well—it was scarcely a pleasure, McCarthy thought, not with those cruel
stewardesses, still one shouldn't be discourteous. *I
was very disappointed with the flight. I found the
stewardesses very . . .* searching for a word, *sharp,
and hard to get along with,* something was faulty
there, what was it? Well—were the stewardesses
sharp or weren't they? Demirgian had said, "Those
stewardesses *aren't* sharp." Essentially affirming
this, McCarthy had somehow lost Demirgian's
negative—a paradox. *I found the stewardesses very
cross,* try it again, *very harsh and hard to get along
with. They were no comfort at all on the flight, and I
feel I should bring this to your attention. Yours truly,*
but the stewardesses didn't have writing paper.

Meanwhile, the plane had landed at Saigon's own
Cimmerian airport, and lo! through the wrinkled
seats of its khaki trousers M company sensed an un-
mistakable gravity pull it to Vietnam's legendary
soil, the root of M's very being. "Gentlemen," a stewardess began, all ladies having timidly deserted
them in Manila, "the temperature on the ground is
84 degrees, the local time is 4:30 A.M. Please remain

seated until . . ." M had no cause to feel in *terra incognita* this morning, lost in the horse latitudes. True: one week earlier, Hofelder could catalog all he knew of Vietnam in three quick sentences, "It's near China. It isn't a very making-money country. The people must eat rice because there's a lot of rice paddies," but in its interlude of filling in mimeographed forms and getting its green steel helmets, in its vast concrete classroom with its infinitesimal sparrows on the heating pipes M had assimilated two full mornings of practical geography; the Army had called them orientations, intending no pun. First, M had seen a distant one-reeler movie. Its grim narrator had observed that the Vietnamese live in an explosive situation, one in which peacefulness does not meet the challenge of today's needs. After the movie a lieutenant had materialized in this tunnel with a map of M's crescent-shaped destination: it was tinted red in its communist areas, pink in contested areas, and white in areas where the Vietnamese had freedom, and it looked like the splotchy diseased liver of some rabbit that the sergeants who taught jungle survival classes had told M don't eat. The same remote lieutenant had then screened some Kodachrome slides, the front row whistling loud and lecherously at six Vietnamese nymphs in those pretty pink and blue things of theirs, the lieutenant's oral caption to this being that Saigon was VD City. Next a prim little captain from the medical corps had taken up Vietnam's endemiology, telling M that it would encounter environmental dangers that had attendant the need for individual adjustments if M was to meet these dangers successfully, the captain absolutely screaming this as *a-r-r-r*, the fiendish ground crew of a super sabre jet fighter tested her wild-blue-yonder faculties with one terrible nearby roar. The captain had screamed rapidly, to get through his dangers in one fleeting hour. He screamed to M that...

...they've got rabies. "Everyone's told you the bad things—I'm going to tell you the good things," said a Negro sergeant who M later applauded, one soldier even shouting hooray and Sullivan even laying aside his *I'm the Last Kamikaze Pilot Alive* to pay close heed. "There's a lot of good-looking girls in Vietnam," the sergeant explained. "I want you to go out of the Capitol hotel! Make a left! One block—make a left! Half a block, cross the street, don't get hit by a taxi—first bar on the right! The Black Cat! Ask for Judy and tell her I sent you," environmental dangers be damned.

From a red-faced master sergeant with the voice of a squawky ten-dollar public-address system, M had heard an extraordinary talk: extraordinary, for in two full months of basic training, two of infantry training, no other sergeant had addressed himself to this vital matter—how to avoid dying. With a decisive *click* the sergeant had turned on a Kodachrome and stated, "This is a punji pit. Now each of those bamboo sticks is sharp—is *sharp,* and there is buffalo dung on every one. There are thousands of these punji pits in the country! *You— will— see them!* What advice can I give you against them? *Don't— fall— in them!*" Click. "This next is a punji foot-trap. Now each of those sticks is barbed—I said is *barbed!* When the medic tries to remove one, it might just *smart!* Just a *bit!* There are thousands of these in Vietnam! *You— will— see them! Don't— step— on them!*" Click.

The sergeant had many further words to the wise and eagle-eyed but no advice against the sudden mortars or mines, the inconspicuous mosquitoes or scorpions—or the cobras. "There's a little one they've got there called Mr. Two-Foot," he stated loudly. "If he bites you in the thumb, *don't* reach in your pocket for a razor blade or a knife! If he bites you anywhere *lie— down— quickly!* Because you're dead!"

Everyone's told you the bad things. Don't go petting the dogs. And don't— fall— in them. Each of these travel tips had been another revelation to Williams, the Negro boy whose innocent civilian wits had never foreseen hazards that he couldn't just avoid by keeping in a low crouch. "You guys don't want me in Vietnam—I'm a coward," Williams announced when the last day of orientations was over, exaggerating the state of mental awareness that it had brought him to.

"Well: we're all cowards," one philosophical soldier replied.

"Look at it this way," Williams again. "We're walking along. We're supposed to keep quiet. I see a boa constrictor standing up on his belly I'm going to *scream. . . .*"

. . . At 4:30 in the morning as Williams exited the plane at Saigon's black airport, there were no boa constrictors on the ramp. M walked across the dark concrete field without encountering punji pits. In a way, Demirgian was sorry about that, disillusioned that on the bottom side of earth the grass seemed to be green and space was Euclidean. It seemed such a waste! Flustered stewardesses, $30,000 pilots, all that expenditure of high-octane fuel and still someone could say and did, "There's the Big Dipper." Demirgian wished it were anything else, the Southern Cross or Halley's comet or anything to make crossing half the lines of longitude a bit more glamorous.

"No, I think it", the G

were everywhere, Americans in gray uniforms, Americans in gray trucks and jeeps. Daylight came, a little American captain bicycling by, bibbidy bobbidy, riding it one-handed to keep returning salutes, and Sullivan said to Demirgian, "What a fairy—what a fink," phrasing the sentence same as he would in the United States. M went to the brown building and filled in mimeographed forms, then it ate master menu in which the scalloped potatoes had been deleted and creamed potatoes had been substituted. M company had come to Vietnam.

Within hours it would go up country. An earnest sergeant said to M, *"Keep alert!"* as M hoisted its duffel bags and itself onto a big open-topped Army truck. "If we pass somebody on the road, if he has something in his hand, I don't care if he's this tall or that tall, girl, boy, it doesn't matter, look to see what it is! And if you don't know, bring it to my attention—*fast,"* looking M square in its squinting eyes. But candidly, as M drove through the bumpy outskirts of Saigon with their outboard motor *put-put* traffic sounds and cooking smells, as M rode to the hinterlands standing, squatting, and sitting on its duffel bags in its airy truck, M could see about fifty thousand persons to its right and left and forty thousand of them had funny things in their hands, wooden boxes, yellow wickerwork baskets, bottles of—*what?* crockery bowls. Twenty thousand people were hurrying by with little twitchy steps—suspicious. Another twenty thousand were standing still—that was worse. On one garbage-congested street, a child without pants who seemed to be playing with empty beer cans rolled one beneath M's truck, M never giving it serious thought. Asia or America, to see a conspiracy in every hand and handbag—that way madness lies, one might as well enlist in the Birch society. A curious fact is that M wasn't armed, the *"Keep alert"* sergeant having no rifles to issue it. M's steel helmets were still ambiguous bulges in its duffel bags, and though there were spare helmets in the truck, their rust had stuck them together and some soldiers had none while others had three, one on top of the other like a little Chinese pagoda. "I know," the earnest-eyed sergeant had said to M, aware that he couldn't fight America's national mania—"you've never seen the scenery, you'll want to look around," and there he had spoken true, the only recalcitrant on this Saigon-and-its-environs sightseeing bus being that boy of sixteen, wild-eyed Russo, who carried a bowie knife long enough to use in dueling and shouted over his shoulder, *"Stay awake, fellas—here comes another hay wagon,"* and other no less faintly ridiculous things. *"I got my eye on that guy,"* he yelled to his unconcerned friends as one young pedestrian took a cylinder no bigger than a cigarette from his black pajamas, set it on fire, and smoked it.

The bustling people, the blue-and-yellow taxis, everything in Vietnam seemed to be about two-thirds of life size, and their colors concentrated as at amusement parks. "Looka! This is like Coney Island without the rides," one soldier cried in an ecstasy of apt identification as Saigon's little brown splinter-board shops with their

_____ bags setting down, squeezing
M's feet, trapping M's feet, the tires roaring, the dust
rising, from out of the tall grasses the communists
would rush, the band would be ambushed one month
later, the French horn, flute, and baritone player
shot, the drummer escaping unscathed—and M
drove gaily past the high barbed wire and into its division's camp.

Imagine anything: now color it dust, red dust, and
that was M's division seat, the size of a practice battlefield. M's old dust avenger, fierce Milett, would
surely go berserkers here, for dust was on every canvas tent, red dust lay on the sandbags, the punching-
bag-shaped water bags, red dust was on every soldier
a minute after his reaching here. The temperature
was maybe 100 degrees. Climbing from the truck
and trudging to some designated tents, M dropped
its duffel bags on its narrow cots as *whoosh!* pillars of
red dust rose from the canvas, and going tardily outside again it waited—waited. Russo began to look
like a short round man in a sauna bath. He sat on the
dusty ground and said, "I'm going to write a letter.
Dear sergeant. You were right. It is hot."

Yoshioka came to have a complexion like a bar of
wet laundry soap. He turned to the *"Keep alert"* sergeant and asked, "Any action around here?"

"Oh no," Demirgian answered him. "It's very
quiet."

"Shit. What do *you* know?" Yoshioka said, his

word collapsing slowly like an unstrung balloon—but M company had an answer soon enough.

"Fall in!" And as M formed ranks in the sunlight a buck sergeant made it deafeningly clear that the joyride was truly over. Like artillery fire his commands hit M one after another, "Troops! Atten . . . tion! First rank, right . . . face! Forward . . . harch! Troops . . . halt! Right . . . face! Second rank, left . . . face! Forward . . . harch! Troops . . . halt! Left . . . face!" until he had M deployed in a line perhaps as wide as a city street. "Forward . . . harch! Route step . . . harch! Troops . . . halt!" he ordered, and M was up against the camp's barbed wire, standing there in the 100 degrees, staring out at what perils God only knew, waifs at the wire of a concentration camp wondering *what now?* And then the sergeant gave the command Demirgian almost dreaded to hear. The sergeant shouted, "About . . . face!"

About face! In two crammed months of basic training, Demirgian hadn't had trouble with right face, it was child's play, or left face, a walkaway, and dress right dress—a lark! the guys all bashing each other around with the Army's jolly consent. But about face—that had been a dark and mystifying thing. Whenever his drill sergeant had given his alarming order *about* . . . Demirgian had shifted faintly to his left foot, and *face,* Demirgian had slipped his right foot behind it, had risen on the tiptoes of both black boots, had swung himself daintily around and—*aww! why didn't it work?* For it didn't ever (try it). Old Sergeant Tisdale, Demirgian's haggard mentor in basic training, a frail and gray-cheeked career soldier, had manifested patience—patience. A graduate of the local school for sergeants, he had earned his Smokey-the-bear drill sergeant's hat by learning to bellow *forward . . . march* in three distinct syllables that wouldn't be mistaken for *port . . . arms* and to scream *right . . . face* in two syllables lest a soldier

with way in his

...Demirgian reporting in, Tisdale had stood him on his royal-blue scatter rug, a $2.98 scatter rug he had bought at Sears so that the Demirgians of this world wouldn't leave any ugly scuff marks as they writhed to the right, left, and about on his office's linoleum, and in his high quick squeaking voice the sergeant had told Demirgian his magic word. The word was youwilltakeyourright-footandplaceitapproximatefourinchesbehindyour-leftfootandslightlytotheleftofyourleftfootandpivot-onehundredandeightydegreesontheheelofyourleft-footandtheballofyourrightfootturningtoyourright. Demirgian listened attentively, then he rose rooster-like on his toes and—*no no no*, Tisdale had said, *listen again*, his voice getting shriller, his patience start-ing to churn up and whitecaps appearing, his con-science whispering to him, *Bambi, your daughter, she's mucking up her fifth-grade homework tonight*, she couldn't do fractions, he wasn't home to help her—Demirgian's fault. Despairing, Tisdale had broken his cabalistic word in twain, he cracked it in two less labyrinthine halves, he screamed it by the numbers, *one! p . . . two!* all in vain, Demirgian still turned like any gauche civilian. Demirgian came to hate the sergeant. Demirgian wanted to kill him, to push him down the black barracks stairs, it wouldn't be difficult—or a bayonet in his withered tummy, *aargh!* When he left basic training, when Demirgian took up infantry at M, nothing had changed—oh, the electric switches in his new barracks were black instead of sickly green, there were other names on the bed frames and it wasn't masking tape but scotch tape that fastened them to the steel, but *about face* was still just *one! p . . . two!* a countdown to spastic disaster, ready, get set, stumble! Once, Demirgian was shown a movie on close-order drill, the narrator, Murrow, called it a symbol of discipline, Demirgian saw undisciplined armies falling all over their bootstraps, Belgian civilians in helter-skelter land, Chinese, who couldn't about face, lying like pick-up-sticks in the streets of Shanghai dead or unhappy-looking, Demirgian just couldn't buy it but there was Murrow intoning, *discipline—discipline— discipline,* you've got to have *discipline* if you're to become s— but there the film had broken. And here was Demirgian at high noon in the combat zone, a sergeant screaming at him, "About . . . *face!*"

Demirgian turned around.

"All right—" the sergeant roared. "Move out! Pick it up! Get it the first time you needn't do it again!" and M disposed itself onto its first professional mission on Vietnam's red soil, Demirgian picking up two small cigarette butts, Yoshioka getting an old match, and Sullivan slinking off left obliquely to his still-dusty tent, a minute ahead of his comrades in arms.

That night M lay on its taut canvas cots and listened to noises—*o-o-o-o-o* things going over and *crump* exploding, *ta-ta-ta-ta* machine guns, automatic rifles, dive bombers, *a-a-ark* tropical birds, lions and tigers, banshees, the spheres of the heavens rolling against each other like empty oildrums, the stars falling and bouncing along the ground: and M company wasn't afraid. Experience had anesthetized it to these sounds of battle during its winter of Army training, its many years of John Wayne. M guessed that all of this racket was American-made

cot.

"Jade East—I like it," Demirgian explained while the cannons and mortars kept up their *o-o-o-o-o*'s and *crump*s.

"Oh. I like Canoe," Sullivan said.

"I don't," Demirgian said. "It smells like dead roses."

"I like Old English," Sullivan said.

"I don't like that," Demirgian said. "I don't like English Leather either."

"I meant English Leather. I like that," Sullivan said.

"I don't like that," Demirgian said. "It's getting too common."

"I use Brut regularly. That's mine," Sullivan said.

And *CRUMP!* The tent tottered as Russo calmly declared, "That's a mortar." M's division had started to rummage for communists in the no-man's-land a few yards beyond M's inky-black sleeping area.

"Mother," said Sullivan, not very disturbed. "Hey, take it easy on my bed."

"Some guys like to play cowboys and indians," Demirgian added. "I like to play this," but he spoke a bit louder than he needed to. If truth be told, Demirgian was getting a little scared: it took a man of vision to turn reality about, to see that equations of parabolic flight must bow to parity, that a whistling can of TNT could go both this-a-way and that-a-way and that M's uneventful side of the barbed wire might someday have its special *crump*s. Soon, Demirgian would learn to exorcise his anxieties the poet's way, on the cardboard wrappers of C-ration cans he would learn to write cathartic verses, one of his rhymes ending, *"You hear the fear yet never shed a tear, every morning . . . every morning . . . every morning."* But tonight, Demirgian took a sip of J&B from a pint pocket bottle and he turned up his transistor radio, its music protecting him from Vietnam's alien noises, eau de cologne from its dusty smells.

"I got the *freight— train— blues,"* Demirgian heard from the armed forces radio station back in Saigon—*crump!* "Lordy lordy lordy, I got them to the bottom of my rambling *shoes. . . ." crump!* The commercials were for US Savings Bonds and for God.

> *Doesn't it get a little lonely sometimes*
> *Out on a limb*
> *Without Him . . .*

"The *pre* . . . ceding," the radio announcer cried, "was presented by— the Armed— Forces— Chaplains Board!" *Crump!* And so it went on M's first night at war: the radio, the tinkling of dog tags as M turned in its sleep, soldiers snoring, and things that go *crump* in the night.

At 4 o'clock M was awakened to go on KP. Demirgian was incredulous: and asking himself when in his slow advance toward the cannon's mouth the folderol would cease, if ever, he authorized himself to march M to the murky kitchen, crying in his outraged voice, "Close it up there! Guide around that sandbag! Got to spit-shine your boots tonight! Got to polish your brass! There'll be a diagram tonight, how to lay out your duffel bag! Hut! two three four. . . ." *Crump!*

all— *Operation,* but truth, of course, wasn't being told, it was classified information, a keepsake given to those with the need-to-know, intelligence and operations officers whose busy wooden desks had imperturbable souvenir signs like: THE SECRECY OF MY JOB PREVENTS ME FROM KNOWING WHAT I AM DOING, and to pale enlisted men whose clickety typewriters and mimeographs totally bespoke the talents for which the Army had given them their high security clearances. Call it coincidence, but eight thousand miles beneath M's glistening combat boots as it graduated from training, eight thousand miles beneath its *tap-tap-tap* as the band played *over hill, over dale,* the mimeographs at this dusty division camp had started to roll, the Operation had become an official order, an obligation on every man in M's division to make the undependable flow of time follow a predetermined course. But when would the Operation be? where would the Operation go? what would the Operation do? The facts were a secret secret—*shh!* Like a secret recipe that is spread between two tasteless slices of bread, the when-where-whats of the Operation lay in a sandwich of mimeographed papers of which it may be said without breaching security: that the first page was stamped SECRET and the last page was signed by the General's adjutant in his grand Hungarian hand.

By Major Sajo. A man of muscle and bone, a man whose skin had been wound upon him as tightly as an Ace bandage and on whose nerve strings one might competently pluck out Bruch's *Violin Concerto in G minor.* Grim determination had made Sajo major while the rest of his class from the Point were still humble company commanders. Count upon it, Sajo's wide shoulders shall someday wear silver stars, he'll be remembered in song and story as the man who filled the Army's arteries with molten steel in some indecisive war of the 1970's by uttering a brave variation on "Praise the Lord and pass the ammunition," on "England expects every man to do his duty," or on *"Ils ne passeront pas,"* a cry of emboldening resolve that his mind may be structuring even now, against the inevitable day. The pity is that this year this man of the hour was in a khaki-collar job, in which his energies could only be squandered by tearing the discomedusan fibers of the blue mimeo stencils that an adjutant has to sign one hundred thousand million of every day. But every Mississippi finds an ocean to spread itself into, and Sajo had found an arena in the dusty red wastes of M's new division camp. Sajo was the moving spirit of the admin company officers club.

BY ORDER OF THE COMMANDING GENERAL: A. J. Sajo. And laying down his stylus with a decisive *click,* Sajo today directed his virile steps to that magnificent club of civilized dining and drinking that he had raised from the desert dust, a Babylon, an Angkor: and Sajo passed through the bamboo curtain at 11:55. No geographical metaphor, this was a real curtain of bamboo beads, a door whose tintinnabulating members he had bought in Saigon and had had painted with the division's red emblem. Characteristically, Sajo had gotten a PFC painter by endowing the assistant chief of staff with a rickety swivel chair that he had inherited from a jet pilot by yielding up a carton of C-rations, the flyboy giving the C-rations to a Vietnamese girl in return for— in return, the girl

⌐wᴏᵣᵉᵤ, ᴵᵉˢ, in return for a sky-blue parachute that he had bequeathed to the General to serve as a shady canopy over his picnic table—*thanks*, and here is your plexiglass. It now was 11:55 and a few seconds.

"Sir?" From behind the washable bar a nervous company commander was speaking to Sajo, rotation having made him bartender on this noontime shift. In his fist the company commander held a bottle opener.

"Beer, thank you," Sajo said to him quietly—never did Sajo unlock his glottal gates lest his animal energies escape in one awful leonine roar.

"Beer coming up," the company commander said.

And curling his fingers around a pilsner glass that the Falstaff people had sent him, Sajo took a slow—slow— satisfied draft, and staring about he feasted his eyes on this solid realization of his resolve, the fruit of his indefatigable labors. Sajo saw that the admin company officers club was good. One thing and one thing alone the home of the admin badmen needed. It needed a real bartender.

Lunch being served by some privates, Sajo strode to his personal table, the *herrentisch* that no ambitious officer had higher aspirations than to eat master menu at. Once, a lieutenant new to Vietnam's folkways had plumped himself at Sajo's sacrosanct table without even a by-your-leave, a cold Mongolian wind blowing through the whole aghast gentlemen's club and Sajo telling this rustic lieutenant, "Find another place to eat," *"You're sitting at my table,"* he once announced to Johnny Unitas, a guest of M's mortified division. At 12 o'clock Sajo sat down there, as yet unaware that the desperate strategy of one of M's soldiers had fixed upon 12 as H-hour and this crucial table as target-for-today. At this historical hour Sajo was approached by a KP waiter for whom his seigneurial presence could hold no terrors, the KP having practiced—practiced all of that morning until he could do expertly even in Daniel's den. From a professional eighteen inches to the right of Sajo's square shoulders he poured him a glass of apple juice: and Sajo looked at the KP surprised. Never had he known an enlisted man to serve apple juice except like a relay runner who is thrusting his wooden baton to the anchor man.

The assistant adjutant was at Sajo's table this fateful afternoon. He asked the KP, "What do you have for lunch?"

And the waiter answered, "Southern fried chicken, sir!"

And the assistant adjutant smiled, saying, "Southern fried chicken—well! You've made it sound good! Most of the waiters would've said . . . *chicken.*" He pronounced it as scornfully as Yoshioka said you-know-what.

And the waiter answered, "Thank you, sir!"

And then—and then as history held its breath the heavens over Asia parted and the voice of providence issued from Sajo's decisive lips. "Soldier, what is your MOS?" Translation, *"What is your job in the Army?"*

"Sir, I'm an eleven-B," *"Sir, I'm a rifleman."*

"Would you like being a cook?"

"Yes sir."

"Would you like being a bartender?"

"Yes sir."

unpredictability from the even tenor of his ways would realize itself on his first full day in the combat zone, the Colt retiring from his nervous hands and a bottle opener replacing it—*moral:* all things come to those who stand and wait. Sajo having changed his MOS to that of a cook and taught him to mix manhattans three to one, an Army career of unimagined civility opened to McCarthy's eyes. The only man in M's expeditionary force to be granted asylum from the literal jaws of death, McCarthy was also the only boy to sleep to 10 or 11, to work in his gray civilian slacks and a shirt of checkerboard red, to delight in the fringe benefits of bamboo beads and of *Combat* on armed forces television, and to have officers and gentlemen as his constant collocutors, *"Man! This puts hair on your chest,"* "Yes sir." Within days McCarthy was making better money than any of his pathetic friends in M ever would—yes, better than Smith would make as a second lieutenant: $117.90 a month for being a PFC, $55.20 for quarters, $95.20 for not being single, $50 in bartending fees, $15 to $20 in tips, and $65 combat pay, so much money that he could afford to oscillate the atmosphere over all the Pacific by placing a telephone call to his bride on her eighteenth birthday.

"Hello?"

"Happy birthday!"

"You stinker," Marilyn said to him, understandably surprised.

"*Blank blank blank blank blank blank blank,*"
let us leave to the canvas walls what Yoshioka muttered the next morning when he heard how a soldier
had courted fortune to become a barkeep instead. In
essence, Yoshioka wanted the happy tapster to rear-
range his anatomy in attitudes of unclear purpose
and uneasy execution, and most of M seconded his
complicated motion.

"Me, I'm glad I can't get liquor around here," Demirgian put in. "I'd be drinking all of the time."

"Well, I was stoned last night," McCarthy.

"Yeah. I saw those guys throwing rocks at you,"
Demirgian.

Except for McCarthy, M wouldn't stay at this
dusty headquarters camp—it would fill in mimeographed forms, then it would go by helicopter deeper
into the boonies to its assigned battalion, to the
front-line bunkers where it would be whenever it
wasn't on a *(whisper)* . . . an Operation. M was still
in: the Army called it the pipeline, and at this critical turn in the tubing one other infantryman dripped
out. Commanded by squawk box to hie himself to the
public information tent to be interviewed for a writing job, Bigalow, the smiling soldier of fortune whose
one ambition in Asia was to strike it rich, perceived
he was at a fork in life's road. A year in a line company and he *might* become sergeant, a corporal got
$163.50 a month but a sergeant got $194.10, one and
one-half years of that dollar a day, another share of
IBM. On the other hand, being where the caissons
roll had certain weak points. One thing, Bigalow
hadn't been trained to fire rifles but to work a mortar, a steel contraption the size and shape of a drain-
age pipe out of whose open end Bigalow was to lob
explosives at communist soldiers a mile, two miles

ʊᴜᴜ s-eye, as ghostly as moiré. But every time Bigalow raised his wet pistol to bring this apparition to
earth, his poncho behaved like a sail and Bigalow's
outstretched arm became a boom, it swung to lee-
ward and Bigalow's watery target remained invio-
late of bullet holes. Dripping wet, the skinny
lieutenant in charge of this fiasco had reported back
to a major, a bear of a man whose nickname was Iron
Mike.

"Sir—" the lieutenant had said, saluting, standing
in Iron's office but shrinking into the doorjamb, a haven with the added advantage of holding him at rigid
attention—"Sir, the men couldn't grasp the pistol."

"What do you mean, couldn't grasp? It's your job
to teach them!"

"I did, sir, but the men couldn't *grasp* it. . . ."

A real dilemma. Bigalow sought out the serious-
eyed *"Keep alert"* sergeant to ask his advice. "I don't
know why *anyone* would want to be on the line," the
sergeant said in amazement—he had been there for
months. "You don't care about being wet because
you're never dry. Your clothing rots. You reach in,
pull out your undershirt and throw it away. And
you're being shot at. And wounded. And when you're
healed and I mean half healed you're sent right back
to the line."

"Yes. But do you make rank?" Bigalow asked.

"I say better to be a live corporal than a sergeant
who's dead. Think about it—think about it."

Bigalow continued to ponder about it, though when he walked into the public information tent and handed his yellow biographical record to a captain at a dusty typewriter, the captain just shouted, "You went to Arizona! I went to Nevada!" and Bigalow could ponder no further. Ten minutes later, the happy former mortar man reappeared at the tent where the rest of M was stuffing its duffel back in its dark green bags, Bigalow smiling mindlessly and saying, "Hey—did you hear? I'm going to be a newspaper reporter."

"Coward," said a jealous unconverted mortar man, continuing to pack.

"I bet I get more medals than you do!"

"Yeah, a yellow one for being yellow."

"The enemy was all around me!" Demirgian began to cry in mock heroics, for he was ashamed of a friend so tolerant of tedium as to stay where he sometimes would pick up cigarette butts and do KP. "All around me! And all I had was my Lindy ball-point pen. They lunged at me. . . ."

". . . They pinned me to the wall!" another boy continued. "I pulled out my ball-point pen! I stabbed! I stabbed! I stabbed. . . ." and then M climbed on its helicopters, its duffel bags in the center aisles like a string of gristly sausages, and it rose deafeningly towards the north as Bigalow the public relations man and McCarthy the Irish bartender stayed behind in their sanctuary.

...ng, and in this idyllic place M seated itself in an arc on the dappled ground to hear its battalion commander, a lieutenant colonel, a light-skinned Negro with shining eyes, welcome it to its journey's end, to its 1966 home. "I know you've heard about this battalion—what've you heard?" the colonel asked, leaning forward for a reply. One hand rested tensely on his pistol holster, the other on his canteen case, not a stance to encourage a frank answer— answer wrong, and it seemed he might fire from both hips at once, *bang! squirt!* the fastest draw in the East, his idiot respondent falling over wet and dead. "Now, I *know* you've heard about us, out with it!" the colonel said—he was known throughout his battalion as Colonel Smoke.

How to answer him? One attentive weekend in Vietnam and M had learned, from the mimeo boys, that this battalion's fate was to encounter the Charlies everywhere, its casualty rate was something wild—it was the jinx battalion, so word of mouth proclaimed. Furthermore, in that edifying weekend M's sharp ears had learned of the Operation itself: that on Monday next, its whole ill-omened battalion was to get on its helicopters and go into Charlie's heartland, go behind Charlie's lines, for seven days M would walk through the Michelin rubber plantation, the same inferno where a regiment of Vietnamese had been annihilated when M was learning its right shoulder arms. Not very surprisingly, M had become privy to the Operation even though the mimeographed order for it was marked, SECRET.

"You!" said the colonel, turning his fiery eyes on one of M's mortar men.

"I heard— sir, I heard you've had most of the action."

"You heard we got killed and wounded, *didn't* you? But you also heard *this,* didn't you? That we killed a lot of VC! And there's no battalion in Vietnam that has *killed* as many VC as we have! And this is our job in Vietnam, we're here to *kill* the VC," M listening silently, none of its faces revealing whether the colonel's words had reassured it. "Now this battalion is good—know why? Why, because we help our buddies. We don't let our *buddies* down. I want you troops to say, if there's *anywhere* in the world I want to get wounded it's in this battalion! Because my *buddies*'ll bring me in, they're not going to *leave* me," M not moving an eyelash. "And this isn't just on the battlefield! Even if you're on KP and don't do it, then who has to do it? Your *buddy!* Suppose—if you goldbrick, if you get VD, if you get yourself sick, then who's got to do your job? Your *buddy!*"

Where, Sullivan asked himself, and Demirgian's lady-chasing friend's train of thought went swerving onto the sidetrack that the colonel had indicated. *Where* in this forest primeval could anyone get VD? and Sullivan peered through the bowers fascinatedly. Already the colonel had oriented Sullivan to his snug situation: his battalion was part of an iron circle, its radius a mighty mile and a half, spirals of barbed wire transfixed its perimeter, trip wires abounded, *Charlie, beware of mines,* artillery now was zeroed in, super sabres and skyraiders knew the coordinates, in a sturdy sandbagged bunker Sullivan was to stand glaring at no-man's-land through a cautious slit, all the arsenal of America's genius at his fingertips, rifles, machine guns, recoilless rifles as

lieutenant colonel. A weird war.

"Now in this village are *whores,*" the colonel continued. "And they're VC whores. And they've got VD a hundred percent. And you've brought fine young healthy bodies here, you'll want to take healthy bodies home to the States. You'll not want to bring *filth* to your wives or the girls you'll marry. And something else about whores! I said you're here to kill VC. Well, there is another reason: you're here to win the minds and hearts of the Vietnamese to loyalty to their government. And you're not doing this if you're chasing *whores.* You're not doing this if your uniform's sloppy, if your shirttail's out," the colonel warming to the topic closest to his heart, the mania that he was named Smoke for, "if your button's unbuttoned. If you don't shave, if you don't cut your hair, the Vietnamese will call you just what you are: a *bum,* and a bum's a bum anywhere in the world, especially so in the East, and . . ." five minutes more in this evangelistic vein and the colonel disappeared, *poof!* in a flash of fire, leaving M standing in line at the adjutant's pretty tent to fill in mimeographed wills.

Nobody spoke much. It wasn't just Smoke's fire-and-brimstone speech that now subdued M, it was also the sudden unearthly silence that he left behind him in this arcadian place. Sullivan stared at the leafy treetops, then at his wristwatch, thinking, *I should get a new strap, this one is falling apart.* Demirgian stood asking himself how long, how *long* would the Army's fashion-consciousness abuse his patience, Demirgian playing with a rubber band and finally snapping it lightly on Morton's neck.

"Now *where* did you get that?" Morton asked him pleasantly, laughing a little, turning around. That was Morton's way—always agreeable no matter what, had Demirgian sunk a stiletto into his neck his response would've been the same, "Now *where* did you get that," had Demirgian shot a rifle round into his cervical vertebrae, wound the sling around his throat, and tugged it with might and main, be assured that Morton would have gasped politely, "All right now, enough's enough," before expiring with a smile. Umbrage just wasn't one of Morton's humors, Morton felt no basic need to assert himself since he didn't believe there was a side to human nature so scoundrelly as to do him harm. Probably he was blessed—definitely Morton was pleasant. A worthy friend for Prochaska, going with him to Times Square and copying his courtesy in giving the Vietnik lady her leaflets back. A few Fridays earlier, when M's compassionate first sergeant had given it its last farewell passes, the sergeant had refused one to Morton, telling him with melancholy basset eyes, "Son, you're not going to *Texas,* not on a three-day pass," and Morton had gone complaisantly to his iron bed, where a dozen friends, a sergeant even, had crowded around him urging him to sign to Trenton, to Philadelphia, to anywhere and go to Texas, *shh!* but Morton had merely chuckled, saying it wouldn't be right. Downstairs on the dayroom's sofa the captain, first sergeant, and operations sergeant were cudgeling their wits to try to intuit whether a man might really fly to Texas and back on a three-day weekend.

"We did it up in thirty-six hours," the operations sergeant was telling them, coming to the point of his

                      and his first sergeant, the three leaders at last putting their faith in this shrinking planet and summoning Morton downstairs in mid-afternoon, giving him a three-day pass to Forth Worth. Arriving there in time for dinner and taking his librarian mother for an evening stroll, Morton had reported to her that he was leaving for Vietnam and to bury him in a silver coffin with a pea-green velvet lining if he should die.

"How you talk!" his mother had replied, but Morton had gone pleasantly on, never supposing that an early death as a teenager was a prospect that he might reasonably be peeved about, as well as routinely concerned with. He said to tell the funeral parlor no shoes, but to consign him to his grave in his black one-button continental suit, a black-dyed carnation in its lapel, his white ruffled formal shirt, and a black bow tie around his neck, against which Demirgian was now snapping a rubber band two feet long.

"Oh! how you talk!" Morton's mother had said.

"Now, *where* did you get that?" Morton asked Demirgian.

"Where do you *think* I got it? From a rubber tree," Demirgian answered, indicating a tree trunk from which a putty-colored glue was rather disturbingly oozing—for that's what the "sycamores" were, rubber trees, and M's new bosky home was a rubber plantation: and the Vietnamese in the village did the tapping, providing American motorists with rubber tires and killing American lieutenant colonels evenings.

In this and every battalion there are three rifle companies, and M was in Vietnam to help bring all three to strength. After willing his $10,000 to his father, Morton was sent to one company, Demirgian to another, Williams, who didn't like boa constrictors or foxhole brims, to a third—M, in whose warm plasma each of its little coagula had felt eternally cared for, M was being pulled apart like a taffy-ball by some unconcerned clerk-typist. New boys at the boarding school, girls at the "get-acquainted" dance on the lonely squeaking chairs, strangers in a strange land, M's quiet privates went to their sunless bunkers one by one. The old soldiers laughed—how they laughed, they doubled up, they tummy-clutched, they looked at M's name tags and har-har-harred. "Hey Sullivan! You an Irishman?"

". . . Yes."

"You better be with a name like Sullivan! Har har har! And *your* name: Demon?"

". . . Demirgian."

"Virgin? Your name is *Virgin?* Har har har!" Above, with a noise like a flapping sail a helicopter with a red cross on its breast was flying by. "Hey look! There come a few more bodies in! Har har har!"

"Har har har! I guess he is really hauling one!"

"One my ass! Har har har!"

And if I laugh at any mortal thing, 'tis that I may not weep. The old-timers were not being cruel on purpose. Half a year—they'd been in Vietnam one half year, a month ago there'd been an ambush, the private they'd given their C-ration cookie to was dead, a man in everyone's squad was dead or wounded: and these, of course, were the empty jungle boots that M was filling. This afternoon the old-timers had given themselves ~~~~ ~~~

~~~~~~~~ ~~~~~~~, but mostly with smooth-skinned children who giggled and tweaked their ears and exorcised all thoughts of war. A source of innocent but intoxicating merriment.

"Girlsan: this beer warm. No good! Number ten!" Colloquy between the two great cultures of Vietnam is held neither in Vietnamese, as the Americans imagine, nor in English, as the Vietnamese infer. The two converse in Japanese, a language where *san* is mister or miss and *ichiban* is number one—the best. "Girlsan: beer number ten!"

"Beer number one! *You* number ten!"

"And *you* babysan of Ho Chi Minh."

"No Ho Chi Minh! He number ten! Number one thousand! You *dien cai dau,*" real Vietnamese meaning loco in the coco.

"Girlsan, I no dinky dow! *You* dinky dow . . ." the merry old soldiers going back to their workaday world in the early evening in that unaccustomed euphoria that M had felt so bullied by.

"Monday you come laundry?" some of the girls in the Vietnamese village had asked them.

"No, Monday we go Michelin plantation," some of the veterans had answered.

"Number one!" some of the girls had declared.

One last orientation and M would be totally oriented, ready to pin the tail on the donkey or grab at the golden ring. Here at Demirgian's platoon a final set of directions flowed from the lips of a fatherly old sergeant with a speech impediment, a defect that had rendered him unable to pronounce any of the twenty-six letters of the English alphabet. A southerner, the sergeant had succumbed to a drawl of such virulence that his vowels had become like the wind in old plantation chimneys, his consonants like the rustling of silken curtains: essence with no substance, matrix without matter, the sergeant's smooth flow of words was a warm dessert in which one could scarcely differentiate between the custard and currants. Early in his Army career, the sergeant had become aware that his most exigent utterances had been falling on the ears of his auditors like an alphabetical list of Hawaiian deities, and to compensate for this involuntary obscurantism he had made it his second nature to say each phrase of his glossolalia over and over until the drift of his Delphic meaning started to come across to the troops. Accordingly, even at times when the sergeant addressed himself to the topics of wrack and ruin, blood and guts, as he was obliged to this evening, even at these bloodcurdling times the warmth of his Florida drawl and the easy leisuredness of his repetitions conspired with his loss-of-signal to make him as comforting as a man chewing a wad of 'baccy and reminiscing about the summer when one of his jerseys took a blue ribbon in Chattahoochee. In this lonely hour, no eloquent gift of gab could have reassured Demirgian as much as this orientation by his soothing new platoon sergeant, Sergeant Allen.

Demirgian was standing with six of M's new arriv-

...g as Allen began his soliloquy, and there's no compelling reason to think that he wasn't saying, "Now, we have a critical situation here. We have one of those I say critical situations, there is a serious situation with Charlie here. Charlie now he could be watching us, Charlie could be at the concertina wire and watching now, Charlie could be there now—he really could. Out there Charlie got machine guns, machine guns and Charlie got mortars, machine guns and mortars and Charlie got punji pits. . . ."

"Punji pits." A helpful Virginia lieutenant was at this briefing to interpret some of Allen's more problematical words.

"Punji pits, and they're poisonous, and they're deadly poisonous, and Charlie got mines . . ."

No favorites. Let us interrupt this vesper service to publish one of Charlie's secrets, his 165th engineer group having given it that official classification.

Description of the DH1O *mine. It looks like a big compass. It is 30 centimeters in diameter and 6 to 7 centimeters in width. Its container is made of tin. Its concave surface contains 420 to 450 steel fragments.*

". . . so Charlie got ammunition, Charlie got plenty ammunition. And ever you're out of ammunition, well, say to your squad sergeant got to have ammunition," one of the charms of Allen's style was a happy lack of rigidity, as airily as Ariel he moved from one to another flower of thought, "because here we got plenty ammunition . . ."

Directions. Set the mine on its quadrupod and face it toward the target. Also the mine can be laid on the branch of a tree, on a hill, on the slope of a mountain, or on a river bank to cast fragments at the enemy infantry. Look through the sight to aim the mine at the enemy.

". . . ammunition, here we got plenty of this ammunition and we got plenty of beer, all of the beer you're going to require we got it . . ."

Plug the blasting cap in, and from the back of the mine connect the wire to 18 cylindrical batteries.

". . . fifteen cents for a can of beer and . . ."

BANG! And as Yoshioka ducked and Demirgian's curious eyes turned to the concertina wire to gaze at the black explosion, a few hundred fragments of steel whistled through the evening air, *s-s-s-s-s,* ten to twenty feet on the sunset side of M's new arrivals.

Was it one of Charlie's DH1O's? Or was it just an American mortar shell with a lot less ambition than it should have had? Who shall decide when sergeants disagree? For an hour or two after the controversial cloud of smoke, the sergeants telephoned people ("Did we fire a mortar round? I took it for a mortar round. But if you didn't fire anything but a white phosphorous it would tend to discount that . . ."). But soon the sergeants forgot about the whole peculiar thing, for it had missed whatever its target was and none of M's new front-line soldiers had been killed or wounded.

Walking back to his bunker, Sullivan said to De-

joy itself in these insecure woods of Cochin China? Put it that lavishly more of the good things of life would come to be M's than it or the worried ladies of Fitchburg, Massachusetts, had ever foreseen. One autumn evening in Fitchburg six ordinary ladies that an irresistible instinct was to tie to M by manila umbilical cord—six still undemonstrative ladies had come to Eileen's place to play po-ke-no, a card a lady, a penny a pot, a cut-glass bowl of Hershey candy kisses to sweeten the profit and alleviate loss. For an hour, little wifely talk of diapers and dishes and girlish cries of "Po-ke-no!" had saturated the bright kitchen air, when the providential turn of the eight of diamonds placed a red plastic po-ke-no chip on the last unoccupied space in one of Eileen's diagonals. Eileen cried *"Diagonal"* and helped herself to the special diagonal pot of a dollar and some-odd cents.

In mock consternation Gladys shrieked, "Ooh! Don't let her win!"

Eileen had just smiled. Her hand heavy with its po-ke-no chips, she pointed to the kitchen's o-shaped fluorescent fixture and to God above it, saying, "He's letting me win because He knows, I'm sending it to the boys overseas." To her mystified friends, Eileen explained that her winnings wouldn't go to their usual depository, the slot in the black plastic hat of Huckleberry Hound. Instead, having read of the horrible jungles in Vietnam, of how our innocent children stand like Ugolino up to their necks in their foxhole's mud or sleep in troughs, a can of cold C-rations to gnaw upon and stagnant water to drink, the communists shooting lead at them uninterruptedly while the Buddhists swing GO HOME YANKEE signs at their groggy heads—having read this in Boston's papers, Eileen would do the Christian thing with her po-ke-no take by sending sort of a CARE package to our needy army. She announced to her stupefied circle tonight that she had already settled upon a battalion—it happened to be M's.

Now, never had a topic so extraparietal as Asia been heard over the fruit-flavored sourballs in Fitchburg, Massachusetts, and Eileen's friends were at a loss how to respond appropriately. Shirley tried to make light of it, "Me, I've got enough bills at home!"

Eileen answered, "Well, will it kill you to send them a ten-cent packet of Kool-Aid?"

Gladys said, "Think of how lucky we are to be sitting here—and then think of *them.*"

Out of little acorns—oaks, and from an idea seeded in this arid-appearing soil a thing would grow, a garden of cardboard boxes to whose philanthropic contents much of Fitchburg contributed, the manager of Iandoli's giving the doughboys seventy-two bars of Dial soap, the doctor chipping in one hundred and four sample cans of Quinsana, and Eileen making the midnight sounds of someone gently wrapping at the Chamber of Commerce. Early in her charitable work, Eileen had written to M's battalion commander, "You, more than anyone else, can tell me what you need in that horrible jungle," and Smoke had answered her wisely from his rubber-plantation office, "We have all of the things we need to do our job. Our government, thanks to you taxpayers, sees to that." But his mind was no match for a woman's heart, and soon there dropped upon M's battalion a generous horn of plenty, a daily delivery of paper plates and

plantation had those as well.

Twenty-four hours at this foreign address and M's new immigrants had learned that the American way of life packages easily—that if given enough corrugated containers the quartermaster corps can deliver it to the antipodes, the touch of the entrepreneurial hand, the *ring . . . g* of the magic register, and there in the horrible jungle were Lady Pepperell Percale Sheets. Pioneers on a new frontier, most of M's mothers' sons assigned themselves now to house and home beautification, the Army issuing empty sandbags and M digging into Vietnam's red sandy soil and into its pockets for everything else. Wallpaper it bought at the PX for seventy-five cents a panel, one pretty panel in each issue of *Playboy*. At the Vietnamese village, M bought corrugated tin to make roofs for ninety piasters or seventy-five cents a clattering sheet as well as God bless 'em: footlockers, for $3 each. "Now this is your home here—this is your hole," the probable words of Demirgian's lovable caramel-chewing platoon sergeant, Sergeant Allen. "Anything you do to improve it, it'll improve you. Now this is your home." A shovel in his enterprising hands, Demirgian fell to improving both at 8 the next morning while corps of smiling Vietnamese children waited on him hand and foot, the girls pushing Cokes in his sweating palms, the boys shining his dusty combat boots for a C-ration stick of chewing gum. Not since 1965 had Eileen's husband's shoes been shined by anyone's hands but his own—it was too much money, a quarter.

In Xanadu did Varoujan a stately baraka decree . . . through measureless hours, Demirgian shoveled the sands into his burlap bags. At noon he bought a footlocker, a Vietnamese one whose gold and silvery spangles were to hint of Oriental silks within, instead of just T-shirts the color of jungle green. By afternoon Demirgian was making his living quarters livable by gracing their walls with a pin-up (the centerfold of a sunshine magazine, it instantly made all other pinups in Asia superfluous)—had just pinned this triptych to his burlap bags when a PFC came to Demirgian's pleasure-dome and ordered him to go to the movies, to *Becket.* "Why do I have to go to the movies?" Demirgian asked.

"The sergeant. He said he wants half the platoon to be *gone.* Let's *go,*" said the PFC whose duty was to relay Allen's orders to the forward area.

"Why do I have to go to the movies?" Demirgian turned to another PFC and asked.

"I don't know, you know the Army." And so, Demirgian set down his building tools to help execute the strange command that half of this platoon be gone, trudging to the ammunition tent and sitting on a crate of bouncing betties to pass his first demoralized day at the front by watching three hours of Richard Burton.

Hindsight suggests that Allen had ordered half his platoon to be *on,* not *gone*—on the perimeter, on duty and on guard. Half of M was always *on* on its motherly rubber plantation, the other half had occasional movies and USO shows and it could inform its leisure hours with a trip to the PX (ONLY ONE MOVIE CAMERA PER PERSON) or to the little museum, the library, the chapel, or the enlisted men's club, a stucco plantation house such as the wives of high-society doctors give candlelight dinners in in Ocho Rios.

...and enjoy beer and Coke and such special items as the quartermaster corps couldn't in conscience waybill, their not being part of the American way. Girls of whose virtue there was utterly no question offered to share their time for $2.50 in words of one syllable, watered whiskey, marijuana, and heroin could also be had here but M didn't buy. Interestingly, the profits on these luxury items went to the busy commander of a Vietnamese division. Our allies had a division camping down the road working the same territory as M's, and thus far in 1966 its companies had killed an average of one half communist apiece.

Even in M's first ho-hum week, a mission of dubious military value was to whisk one of its lucky soldiers to Saigon for an evening of it, Eileen wouldn't get to Boston till Christmas. The quick flight to Vietnam's capital was to satisfy this soldier's curiosity whom to believe, the Secretary of Defense who had sworn that the city wasn't an American brothel or the Secretary's lieutenant who had turned on his photographs and nicknamed it VD City. Since impartial laboratory tests were to prove the lieutenant disconcertingly right, let modesty give a *nom de guerre* to this first of M's many reconnoiterers here, and as good intentions carry him on a well-walked road the minutes of his meetings and partings shall call him Legion. Like all of M's innocents, this boy Legion had been oriented to Saigon's pleasures and perils back in his foresighted training camp, the same sergeant who had firmly advised him against the punji pits, *"Don't— fall— in them,"* having warned him about the pitfalls of the rear. "Let's say you're on a trip to Saigon," the sergeant had squawked in his $10 public-address-system voice, "you're sitting there in the Happy Bar. A guy comes in in civilian clothes, he puts a package under your stool. Get up and move! *Move!* Or you're in the streets out shopping and a guy throws a present to you. *Throw it back!* Or at your hotel—a guy parks a garbage truck and he saunters away. *Watch out!* Or a cute little kid on a bicycle leans it against the wall. *It may blow up!* Now in Saigon you can trust no one! No one! Man, woman, or child!" At 6:15 in the evening as Legion began his walking tour of this deathtrap, he wouldn't have ignored the sergeant's recommendations had he seen slitted eyes staring at him from under the manhole covers or heard weird ipcress sounds in the scorching air, but in this busy seaport it seemed to be one more paranoiac's advice. In all, Legion saw a thousand citizens in tinny Lambretta trucks who parked them and strolled away and five thousand characters on bent-looking bikes and motorbikes who leaned them against the peeling walls—so what could a soldier do? Far from wearing his flak jacket, Legion wore his civilian clothes when at this early hour and early age he started upon his circuit of Saigon-by-night. By the clock on the city's tallest hotel it was *6:15.*

6:15. In the middle of Saigon's modest equivalent to the Etoile, Legion sees a blue billboard with a red message, LONG LIVE THE SPIRIT OF MUTUAL ASSISTANCE. This generous exclamation is the epicenter for four broad avenues on which Legion sees a scene of such cataclysmic anarchy that he almost needs a blockbuster bomb to account for it, a thousand tons of TNT that has charitably fallen into the PX and scattered its cellophaned

dressed to a very small businessman, who turns to his mother silently.

"He's an American," the mother says in Vietnamese and keeps on chewing her betel nuts.

"Three hundred piasters," the child says to Legion in finger language—$2.50, and Legion buys a couple of T-shirts in their crispy cellophane wrappers, a necessity that the PX on the rubber plantation is inexplicably out of.

6:30. A sudden differential in the pressure against his toes reveals to Legion that his dusty loafers are being shined by a Vietnamese urchin who breaks into poignant tears when his customer pays him twenty piasters, the urchin spitting on this meager bill and throwing it to the gutter, grinding it in the garbage there. Conscience stricken, Legion gives him another one hundred piasters.

6:35. Offered a real ocelot by a man with a yellow alley cat, Legion buys a genuine vertebrate for twelve hundred piasters, and taking his guaranteed animal into a taxi whose driver doesn't remember to throw the meter he commences to hop to the crowded bars—at the first, kitty was fated to crawl away on all four three-hundred-piaster paws.

6:40. Walking into this first neon-illuminated stop, Legion is recognized by the barman as a soldier fresh from the muck and the mire. *"Yankee!"* the barman cries and he isn't content until he has treated his mutual assistant to two double scotches and joined him in choruses of *The mademoiselle from— correction!* that was some other war. What really happens as Legion walks shyly in, the girl behind the noisy bar identifies him as a soldier fresh from the country and charges him a hundred and fifty piasters for a fluid the color of wonton soup, but colder.

6:41. From under the garish bar, Flower brings out a deck of cards saying to Legion, "We play gin? For double or nothing?" The girl behind the bar's name is Flower or Flour.

"Double or nothing," sporting old Legion agrees.

6:42. Flower says, *"May noi tao nen danh con bai nao? Con ba, con bon, hay con bay?"* Flower has been playing a lady's game of gin by talking a blue streak of Vietnamese to a girl who is standing just in back of Legion's right shoulder.

The girl in back of Legion's right shoulder replies, *"Con bay. No dang cam con ba."*

6:43. Flower announces in English, "I win."

7:40. By now Legion's normal transcendental wish to become as one with his Asian environment has surfaced as a real warmth for Flower herself, a girl whose wide Polynesian smile makes the reciprocity of her emotions practically seductive and whose tiny Chinese figure makes her alcoholic capacity astonishing—Flower is on her eighth incredible jigger of something-or-other as Legion gallantly pays the hundred and fifty piasters a shot.

cused herself to the ladies room, Flower is never seen or heard of again.

8:45. Other bars other loves, and Legion awakes on his rubber plantation four mornings later to find himself *hors de combat,* the very first casualty of M's impetuous expeditionary force. Ah youth! as Conrad would say, Legion had enjoyed every minute of his coming of age in Asia, all of this comfortable week he reminisced about it to the beardless youths who would someday follow his wayward steps to Gomorrah. Of course, Legion's holiday trip had taken him by an uncharacteristic fraction of the Vietnamese. Let it be entered in Legion's diary that ninety-nine percent of these decent people had scorned opportunity by paying him no attention at all—except, of course, by ordering their daughters never to speak with him or his vulgar American ilk.

News is what is unusual. Any morning that Eileen read of a company that had been ambushed she could assume that a thousand companies hadn't been, and every night that the TV had one thousand malcontents crying, *"Down with . . ."* in Saigon she could deduce that 1,990,000 others were staying in their apartments or playing gin. The communist shot and shell that the Boston papers wrote of so vividly didn't disturb the foliage of M's quiet plantation all of this ordinary week, the Vietnamese rubber workers didn't kill a mortal soul and M wasn't ambushed, it wasn't slowly strangled to death by boa constrictors, it didn't catch clonorchiasis. With the cleaning rods of its rifles it drew little *ooo*s in the level earth and with combat boots it erased them, it cleaned its fingernails with the cotter pins of its hand grenades, it ate many fruitcakes. The week before the Operation, M had a very ordinary week.

Let nobody doubt it. If the high priests of Thebes who buried pharoahs were to appear at M's hot dusty division camp, the *hemneters* would be at home among the sights and sounds of the chamber where the staff officers stood in whispering circles to plan for the Operation, silver birds or silver leaves on the collars around their necks. An almost geometrical cube, the sanctum sanctorum was overgrown with the moss of military maps, and on their dark green surfaces the lean and bony-faced colonels drew curving lines in allegoric colors and washed them off with rags dipped in methyl alcohol, the colonels all chanting things like *the hueys in the lima-zulu* with so much familiarity that one might almost believe these were English words. The colonels used the color true-blue for American battalions and for the bolsheviks, orange—the pencil cabinet being fresh out of red. The plan of M's first Operation was: on Monday next, M's idle battalion was to quit twiddling its thumbs, going to movie theaters, and losing its ocelots and to fly by gray-green helicopters to the Michelin rubber plantation's east, an army of Vietnamese colonels and majors and captains having given its ceremonious okay for American aliens to land on these sovereign coordinates but promising to keep the Operation secret. Other battalions had other jobs, but M's was to sweep across the planta-

issuing mimeographed orders, the adjutant putting his A. J. Sajo on the flimsy blue stencils and striding off to his admin company officers club. Getting to his plexiglass bar at 11:30 today, Sajo cried to his chosen bartender, *"Mac,"* and then stretched his fists at the bartender's smiling face as though that menial were a tow-rope and Sajo were water-skiing behind him. McCarthy hesitantly tapping the customer's right fist, it popped open to reveal a white pawn, and Sajo announced to him, "You're white," the major and PFC would be playing chess.

McCarthy was wearing his checkered red bartender's shirt, his Sunday-go-to-the-drag-races charcoal pants. The junior officers were in their gold and silver collar-bars to witness the ritual triumph of him whose dominion here was so totalitarian that he had once roared to a captain whose wet little fingers were cradling a half-eaten peach—had roared across the civilized club to this barbaric captain, *"If you can't eat like a gentleman, get out!"* The game of chess commencing, White now opened with his inveterate caution.

$$\text{Kt–KR}_3 \qquad \text{P–K}_4$$
$$\text{Kt–QR}_3$$

"Very interesting. Very interesting for a young punk," Sajo declared. He had never seen an opening quite so circumspect had anyone—ever?

B–QB$_4$

P–K$_4$ Kt–QB$_3$

Q–B$_3$ Kt–KR$_3$

"I see you've never played against a Hungah . . . rian," Sajo said as he skillfully guarded his bishop's pawn.

B–B$_4$ Kt–QR$_4$

"Yes, obviously you've never played against a Hungah . . . rian," Sajo said as he counterattacked with his queen's knight.

P–Q$_3$ P–Q$_3$

BxKt

"Very interesting. But you've never played against a Hungah . . . rian," Sajo said and he won this speedy exchange.

PxB

QxP

"Checkmate," McCarthy said.

At first, the silence in the home of the admin badmen was so pervasive that the tinkle of the genuine bamboo curtain seemed louder than the temple bells of Mandalay. Then, as Sajo turned the color of a bloody mary a lieutenant whispered, *"Fool's mate."* Other enchanted officers ventured to say it louder, *"Fool's mate."* Delighted lieutenants and captains clapped on the plexiglass and turned it into a shout, *"Fool's mate."* Red, orange, and yellow confetti appeared in their hands, the jubilant badmen threw it and blew themselves purple on paper horns, they stood on their howling heads, they interlocked arms and legs and danced the Cossack *prisyadka*—hey! a banana-split over the roof, a somersault over the wire, a leap in their jeeps and they drove to Hanoi and—*waaaa,* the officers leaned on their horns and shouted across the paddies to friend and to foe alike, *"Fool's mate! Fool's mate! Fool's mate!"*

Sajo said rigidly, "Two out of three," but McCar-

ture a paleíaced tribe of Indians dumping the boxes of *tra* into Boston harbor? Hadn't a man in a red frock pop-art coat arisen in Virginia's halls to cry, *"Tu-do hay la chet,"* and hadn't a rider in a blue three-cornered benday hat galloped to Concord shouting, *"Quan anh sap toi"*? Seizing some typewriter keys, one of the newly brave officers wrote, *"When in the course of—"* well, those weren't his very words but he nailed a proclamation to the two-by-fours which kept the roof of this clubhouse from falling in, the spirit of 1776 prevailing on Friday night when the admin badmen met to elect— a President! One officer nominated the assistant adjutant.

"Freddie, you will decline the nomination!" Sajo roared.

"He's been nominated, he can't decline!" a captain shouted.

"Freddie . . ." Sajo bellowed.

"Sir, you're out of order!" the chairman screamed.

"I nominate the chairman. . . ."

"I nominate the Chaplain. . . ."

"I second the nomination. . . ."

"I rise on a point of personal privilege! I say it's hot in here," the Chaplain exclaimed. "I'd like to get me a drink!"

"The chair will entertain a motion to—"

"I so move!"

"I second it!"

"All in favor of taking a break at the bar say—"

"Aye!"

"McCarthy!" the Chaplain shouted. "Make it a Coke!"

"McCarthy!" a captain ordered. "I'll have a bourbon and branch!"

"McCarthy!" a major commanded. "Give me a crème de cacao!"

. . . And that is why some educational comic book of the year 2066 may well include a four-color soldier from M in the midst of the founding fathers who sowed democratic seed in Vietnam, a bit before midnight electing the Chaplain president of the admin company officers club as Sajo got the bamboo gate. No retribution was to fall on McCarthy's indiscreet head for his first inflammatory act of lese majesty. He kept on working wearing his checkered red bartender's shirt and smiling his "What is the sahib's pleasure" smile. Half of each night he stood at his duty station mixing manhattans three to one, telling the officers that *yes* it put hair on their chests, and waiting— waiting— waiting for a letter from Marilyn that wouldn't come, for Marilyn was suing him for divorce.

Half of each night Demirgian sat on his bunker's roof and glanced at times at the concertina wire in the silver moonlight to assure himself that it wasn't a nest of communist infiltrators. Sounds in the night surrounded him, artillery's *o-o-o-o-o*'s and the mortars' *crump*s, the *ta-ta-ta-ta*'s of imaginative machine gunners, the scary metallic *k-k-k*'s of the rubber nuts popping open, the voices of other sleepless soldier-boys. . . .

"Do you think a man could really rape a woman?"

"Affirmative! Aren't there men strong enough to pin you?"

Clausewitz alone can conceive by what diabolical wiring the communists caused a ten-watt incandescent bulb to wink at Demirgian like a Chinese torture device—psychological warfare. America's *crump*s having failed to extinguish it, Demirgian's company had simply said to hell with the winking wonder; let it wink. The first time Demirgian mounted guard, one of the battle-tested veterans had climbed on Demirgian's bunker with his cigarette lighter high and had shouted to the enemy electricians, "All right! I see *you*—you see *me!* All right?" The neighborly soldier's way with the communists had recommended itself to Demirgian's fancy as fitting and proper—wittily insubordinate, unafraid of Charlie, spirited, stagy, and death-defying.

Demirgian's new sworn enemy (Demirgian had sworn it his first hour in the Army, his right arm raised in a limp-looking L, his feet in a pair of brown loafers, the stars and stripes bearing its silky witness)—Demirgian's new teenaged enemy had taken infantry training at a Northern camp, a camp where his toothbrush and toothpaste were in a small canvas bag. Charlie himself had to sew this ditty-bag on his first chaotic day in infantry training camp. When the tiny drawstring of his finished bag was hooked on the tenpenny nail by Charlie's wooden bunk, the weight of Charlie's toothbrush and toothpaste pulled the drawstring closed and Charlie's pebble-eyed sergeants made it menacingly clear that the string must be closed up tight—tight! But whether the brush in Charlie's canonical bag had its bristles down or its bristles up and whether the brand name on Charlie's toothpaste tube appeared as NGOC-LAN or NGOC-LAN was of no real concern to Charlie's otherwise tyrannical sergeants. Early each morning when Charlie shaved, he had to take his razor apart as carefully as a 45 and place its component parts in a plastic case, the shaving head falling punctiliously to the left, the handle to the upper right, the blade to the lower right—again, the sergeants not giving a tinker's damn if Charlie's segregated blade had the English words MADE IN CZECHOSLOVAKIA rightside-up or upside-down. His comb Charlie carried in his shirt pocket. Charlie's good grooming was a high-priority duty in this Northern camp: and once, a private whose hair was as black as Demirgian's had to sit without saying *ouch* as his sergeant cut off those criminal locks with clippers and plucked out a mustache with a set of tweezers, little black hair by hair—the name of that fiendish sergeant was Tuong, the outrage did indeed happen at the pitiless camp in Hungyen, east of Hanoi. The communist camp didn't have a policy of no molesting trainees.

Charlie's ogreish sergeants couldn't get Charlie to polish his brass since he hadn't any, Charlie couldn't shine his canvas combat boots, but Charlie had to have buttons buttoned and if beneath Charlie's bunk his shoes didn't lie in a line as accurate as those of Olympic sprinters at the start of the one-hundred meter dash, if that didn't happen as Tuong got down on his bony knees and squinted from toe to canvas toe, if this exhibit of shoes wasn't architecturally true—then Charlie would have an angry sergeant.

... would bethink himself of the child that
was father of this scrupulous man and Tuong would
say to Charlie forbearingly, "Comrade, I went
through this myself—I'm glad I did. The army's a
furnace. It tempers a man into steel."

And so, for four months the blast of his drill sergeant's furnace had firmed up Charlie's soft mole-
cules. At the bellow of *nghiem*, Charlie would snap to
the same erect attitude that Demirgian sometimes
assumed when his sergeant commanded *atten* . . .
tion! At the sergeant's roar of *nghi*, Charlie would
pop a knee three inches forward as though he were
doing the first spastic movement of the Haitian
merengue, much as Demirgian went to his usual Cro-
Magnon slouch when his sergeant ordered *at ease.*
Charlie's *ben phai* . . . *quay* and *ben trai* . . . *quay*
were the same wooden-soldier movements as Demir-
gian's *right* . . . *face* and *left* . . . *face*, but Charlie's
dang sau . . . *quay* or *about* . . . *face* was a tarantella
with no real parallel in Demirgian's army, a step of
such corybantic madness that if Demirgian's dark
parents had emigrated from the Caucasus towards
the rising sun instead of the setting sun, it would
take but *dang sau* . . . *quay* for their stumbling prog-
eny to accomplish his heart's desire and be mustered
out of Ho's army as arrantly unfit for military service. Whoever had choreographed the steps of *about*
. . . *face* for Charlie's army had apparently been a
Russian advisor, for he lacked the Oriental virtue of

patient reflection but went about designing an *about
. . . face* as impetuously as a Karamazov. One sus-
pects that the commissar had suddenly hurled himself a hundred and eighty degrees around, and that
catching himself before he could fall sprawling on
the parade grounds he had recommended to Charlie's aghast sergeants that they follow his breakneck
example. More specifically, at the preparatory command of *dang sau* . . . Charlie was to shift his
hundred-and-something pounds to the trembling
toes of his left foot and heel of his right foot, and at
the command of execution . . . *quay,* Charlie was to
whirl to his right on these two points of precarious
balance and recover himself as best he could before
he could make a shambles of the May Day Parade.
The maneuver required of Charlie a real spirit of
I-have-set-my-life-upon-a-cast-and-I-will-stand-the-
hazard-of-the-die. Try it yourself in your living room
but first move the furniture back. At his madcap
training camp, Charlie's mean mousy-toothed sergeant had taken one whole morning to teach him a
skill as peripheral as *dang sau* . . . *quay,* even as
American stratofortresses were blowing up bridges
and train tracks all around. The way Tuong taught
it, Charlie was first to *quay* himself through sixty
little kindergarten degrees of arc. Then after Charlie
had learned to toddle he was to pivot through one
hundred and twenty degrees and ultimately through
all one hundred and eighty. But gradualism was of
small avail to Charlie's Sergeant Tuong. Just three
seconds after he had given his bloodcurdling order
for a full semicircular *dang sau* . . . *quay,* his whole
sprawled platoon seemed to be posing for Delacroix's
Massacre at Chios or Gros's *Murat Defeating the
Egyptian Army at Aboukir.* Everything was arms
and legs, and Charlie was so shattered by this vicious scrimmage that he couldn't be blamed had he
told himself all that aching afternoon, *one of those*

pany even as Demirgian sat in his orpheum listening to Burton say, "My lord, did I tell you? My new gold dishes have arrived from Florence." American artillerymen far beyond Charlie's horizon put aside their Japanese cameras long enough to send their sixty-pound cans of dynamite onto Charlie's ringing ears. Lazy little flights of bombers came by and pilots with a date in Saigon that evening radioed, *uh . . . roger,* in a voice as casual as the corner grocer's. *Today we have twenty-four 750-pound napalms,* I think you'll like our honeydew melons *and thirty-two hundred rounds of 20 mike-mikes. Where do you want 'em today?* For food Charlie's master menu was: rice, and he couldn't cook it for breakfast, lunch, or supper, the fires would show on some sinister thing of Demirgian's scientific army. Charlie's only drinking water was a hepatitisade, the submarine abode of cholera and typhoid germs who wouldn't live a minute in Demirgian's inoculated blood. Mosquitoes gave Charlie malaria, but Demirgian was a man whose heart was pumping twenty-six milligrams of methoxyquinoline phosphate. At night when Charlie lay thinking of the family hearth that he left to become tempered steel, Demirgian sat listening to the armed forces radio station's *if I had a ham . . . mer* and *yeah yeah yeah:* that, or Demirgian was playing whist. In time, Charlie's little toothpaste tube surrendered its final morsel, the last of his properly buttoned buttons popped into the underbrush, his shoes were so disgraceful that if Tuong had inspected them a real hysterical ataxia would have stricken his twitchy little fists. And then one ghastly night as Charlie lay on his torn poncho a phosphorescent skeleton visited him, it danced above the treetops crying to Charlie, *"Hello . . . I'm a lonely communist soldier! I died a thousand kilometers from my native village! Now, I'll never ever be with my ancestors!"* Far above this talkative skeleton, Charlie could hear a hovering helicopter, but by the first light of morning four of his petrified friends had surrendered to Demirgian's satanical army: and told it their anecdotal tales.

Hardship hardens a man. But there at Demirgian's snug plantation, Charlie had few expedients other than Tuong-like huffing and puffing. Charlie couldn't lay siege in the grand Chou dynasty manner, everything came to Demirgian's castle by fat-bellied planes. Twice when Charlie tried to attack it, before he had even blown *charge* he was seen on the radar screen and that ended that. *Crump—crump—* every time a couple of mortar shells fell on Demirgian's carefree estate it meant one of Charlie's pick-a-back boys had carried them all three months through the narrow jungle, the same whenever two of Charlie's DH10 mines exploded. The weeks when Charlie's imperturbable enemies left their asylum and took to the field themselves, Charlie had a wider range of options, but none were Napoleonic. The four rules of guerilla warfare that he had learned in his training camp—when the enemy advances, we retreat, when the enemy pauses, we harass, when the enemy tires, we attack, when the enemy retreats, we pursue—the four simple guerilla rules had withered away in practice to two even easier ones, for the American army never retreated and the Vietnamese army never advanced. Charlie's strategy had become: attack the Vietnamese army and escape the

...ies in ambush and snipers in every yellow village, the idea being that the snipers fire, the American soldiers return fire, a Vietnamese dies and Charlie has good propaganda. And what of the Vietnamese themselves in their pastoral no-man's land? One doesn't know, but a guess is these reticent people felt about this strategy and counterstrategy the same as some characters felt about the lion and the unicorn.

One breezy night as Demirgian sat on his dark cubic bunker, as Charlie lay beyond the barbed wire winking his bulb at Demirgian and impotently waxing wroth—one night of this comfortable week the skies in front of Demirgian's spellbound eyes were a pale orange, it seemed that an Asian metropolis with its neon-illuminated ginzas lay in the rolling hills. That afternoon the napalm had fallen in something dry, a fire had started and spread. In the Vietnamese villages beyond the orange horizon anything might be happening, horses might be running into burning barns, firemen might be wearing red suspenders, emperors might be plucking on samisens, no one in Demirgian's company knew—no one even cared. For to Demirgian's war-waging company there was nothing in the wild orange yonder that was animal, vegetable, or mineral other than— *Charlie.* When a man's in a duel to the death, the pageboys with the purple cushions aren't apt to arrest his preoccupied eyes.

Down to the edge of the rubber trees came Demirgian's round and rather jolly captain, with him a Negro lieutenant, his second-in-command, and both of them looked at the orange skies in approval. "Burn, burn, burn," Demirgian's captain said. "Yes, that'll get old Charlie out."

"Yes sir," the lieutenant said.

"Charlie's got no place to hide now. Charlie don't like open spaces," the captain said.

"No sir, that Charlie don't," the lieutenant said.

"That's the way to end this war. Burn the villages—burn the farms," the captain said. "Then the Charlies'll have to come in planting and rebuilding instead of just stirring up trouble."

"Yes sir," the lieutenant said. "I think we should burn the rice harvest too."

"The fire makes me happy. Burn, burn, burn," the captain said.

"The breeze is really blowing it along," the lieutenant said.

"Yes, feel the breeze. And it'll blow the mosquitoes away," the captain said. "Burn, burn, burn."

"Yes sir," the lieutenant said.

"Indignant at the US commanders' order, two US servicemen shot and killed themselves, two other servicemen disemboweled themselves and died immediately, and three Negro servicemen jumped out of the aircraft to their deaths."

And that's the way the world spins, good night. The tragic "news" that the Hanoi radio station gave to M each evening about its fantastic battalion had an effect on its unseen audience that was to make a mockery of the station's big electricity bill. Nothing in M's busy training had taught it the real evils of communism as crisply as did these propaganda casts of Hanoi Hannah. Clearly, the whole ideology was in

...much a catechism as a public-opinion poll, and M couldn't be said to have *learned.* "As you know," the Captain had accurately begun, his hands in his wool pockets, his Bojangles smile bright white, his eyes flicking over the vast concrete room—"as you know, communism is—as you might say—our competition," but after that one declarative sentence all of the Captain's tutelage had closed with a question mark. His second sentence was, "Who can name the people who laid the roots of communism?"

"Sir. I say Stalin had something to do with it."

"How many people agree? How many disagree?" the Captain had asked, and M had expressed its consensus with a one-sided show of hands. As soon as this method had democratically seated Lenin and Marx in the communist pantheon, the Captain had actually said to M, "Now we've talked about the theory of communism. Now we'll talk about its basic ideas—what is wrong with communism's ideals?"

"Sir. They don't believe in God."

"Sir. Everybody has equal shares, no person owns one thing."

"Sir. When you're old and they've no use for you they'll throw you away or shoot you, while in America they'll send you to an old people's home."

"How many people agree? How many disagree? How many don't know? How many don't give a damn?" M's inquisitive captain had asked it, his plebescite being the length and breadth of M company's inculcation in communism. But the truth is M didn't need to know its enemy to abominate him, just as it didn't need Thomist philosophy to appreciate that God is good. Communism's wickedness seemed to M to be sewn in the primeval warp of the universe, it was indelible like the earth's magnetic field, it was axiomatic: for M had never in its twenty years of life heard otherwise. "How many people," the Captain had asked in his last referendum—"how many people say that communism and the American way of life are opposite?" Even if M could have quoted chapter and verse of *Capital* as effortlessly as its Army serial numbers, M's show of hands couldn't have been more unanimous.

One week later when M was being whisked to the ends of this earth to oppose the communist way, it couldn't have quoted two consecutive words of Johnson's why it was going there: and M didn't need to. M firmly believed—or rather, it firmly believed that it firmly believed—in the principle of perpendicular geography, the article of faith that all of this world's sovereign countries stand on their ends and if one topples over the rest shall follow, that if Vietnam falls to its enemies the cursed tide of communism shall flow across the Pacific as inexorably as the Japan current. M had held forth on this tenet in the course of its airplane trip to Vietnam. It had stopped in Oakland to fill in mimeographed forms when a Vietnik college student, forty to fifty years of age, tried to convert some of M's true believers into going awol or lying down on the runway or something like that. By way of argument the Vietnik said, "Read *The New York Times.*"

Demirgian had answered him *a perpendicula* saying, "The communists win in Vietnam it'll just be Laos, Thailand, the Philippines, and then we'll have to fight in California."

"That isn't true," the Vietnik riposted. "Read *The*

...as ſuly academic as the architectural pros and cons of some gingerbread mansion might be to the fire fighters in its attic trying to save it (and themselves) from annihilation. And since it was utterly irrelevant, the question of *should America be here or shouldn't it* seemed to M to be universally irrelevant as well. It was human of M to assume that an utter irrelevance knew no geographical frontiers and that the logical process of the American people—indeed, that Logic itself—owed it to common courtesy to accommodate itself to M's real presence in Vietnam and to justify the present peril to M's life and limb. M believed that America should believe in M, and M felt betrayed by all acts of Vietnikism: literally betrayed. Prochaska had told himself after being in Times Square, *if we're going to die over there, at least people at home should support us,* and Bigalow was to write the optimistic words *for immediate release* on a public-information poem:

> We've had Benedict Arnold and Tokyo Rose,
> And now we've got Vietniks in raggedy clothes,
> There is only one thought as I'm thinking afar,
> Just who in the hell do they think they are?

And when Congress itself became lost in its tardy *should we shouldn't we* agonies, M company felt—dizzy, to M in its front-line bunkers the Congress's deliberations seemed to go against the order of God's universe, as though from the normal process of cause and effect *cause* was being retroactively plucked and *effect* was being left to go spinning around the world endogenously like a perpetual dust-devil. It seemed to M that if in the busy press of circumstance action hadn't had time to accord itself with thought—if not, then thought should adapt itself to action retroactively.

It was a very human sentiment, and when senators and representatives flew across the waters to M they reciprocated it, they suffered a sea-change when the ethereal concept *the American commitment* took on flesh and bones and materialized in front of their watery eyes as M's noble soldiers. The weekend before the Operation, two chubby congressmen did indeed call on the rubber plantation, one a Texas congressman in a sky-blue siren suit, the other a California congressman in a set of such baggy borrowed fatigues that he could have carried a dozen copies of the 1966 federal budget within it without its acquiring one extra lump. A report of the congressmen's imminence was speeded down to the bunkers through the facilities of the signal corps. Yoshioka being from California, a sergeant now called to him, "Yokasoka! Go get your helmet, your pistol belt! You're going to shake hands with your congressman!" It was rather from a sense of propriety than one of soldierly pride that the Texas and California troops were being ordered to doff their everyday "baseball" caps, to rummage in their duffel bags for their steel helmets and combat gear, and to present themselves to their elected representatives dressed to kill. It wasn't—it *wasn't*—from any conscious wish to pull the wool over the good congressmen's eyes. It was simply—well, war is what they'd junketed here to see, right? and M was just showing the same consideration that newsmen do who rest their pencils behind their ears or between

"Aww sergeant. They told me I could go to the shower point have a shower."

"Listen, do you think your congressman had a shower this morning? If he didn't have a shower why should you?"

"Sergeant, he's not my congressman. I'm from Illinois," said the dusty soldier, but he got himself ready for congressmen or communists nevertheless.

The site of this dramatic operation was to be M's shady battalion command post. Two scant minutes ahead of their sad-sack congressmen, the Texas and California constituents arrived, Morton of Texas wearing a pair of old pineapple hand grenades, the first grenades he had ever owned, Yoshioka of California with a 45. Pandemonium ruled in these usually tranquil woods. A sergeant with no romantic sensitivities ran around the area berserk and cried to himself in disbelief, "You've got to wear a steel pot to see your congressman!" A frantic Negro lieutenant snapped out commands, "Line up, Texas on this side! California on this side! *Sergeant,*" to a man with a squad at such prosy civilian work as sawing wood—*"Sergeant,* hide those workers behind the building! *Soldier,*" to Yoshioka, *"where is your camouflage?"* and faster than a hockey player can be given a new hockey stick the bright new helmet was plucked from Yoshioka's head and a pot with a manly burlap wrapping was plunked on his GI haircut instead—*plunk,* as the congressmen toddled into view. *"Gentlemen,"* a sergeant with presence of mind leapt forward to say, "Texas is on the left! California is on the right!"

Metamorphosis. Up until this spellbinding minute, the congressmen had been chattering happily with a one-star general—up until *the American commitment* appeared in the robust form of America's youth. Then, a moist little look of both pride and shame spread across the faces of America's lawmakers: pride in these gallant men at arms, shame in those of such little faith as to ask if their presence in this suffering country might be for anything but Vietnam's best. Texas walked lovingly down the left-hand line. "Good job . . . good job," he said to Morton and patted him on the shoulder opposite the hand grenades, and California murmured to Yoshioka, "Good . . . good." Then the two chastened congressmen flew to America to make their patriotic speeches, and Morton and Yoshioka retired into the shadows of their poetic plantation to get themselves ready for their test of arms: for Monday morning's Operation.

The woods are lovely, dark and deep—but I have promises to keep.

Am I Right or Wrong?

...perate history, M could experience pleasant weather. The temperature at M's altitude was 70, and through the sides of its swift helicopters there came one of those summer-in-a-sports-car and hair-rumpling breezes. With its whole silent battalion and three battalions more, M was in combat clothes being lifted out towards the Michelin rubber plantation, a forest where the communists, all busy little beavers, had been whittling bamboo stakes, dipping them in buffalo dung, urinating on them, putting them in punji pits, in foot-traps, in mad little Batman traps in trees, *whiz!* out of bushes, *pop!* out of ferns—*aargh!* and burying mines and hiding grenades and *"Here it comes,"* as M had once heard from grinning old Foley back in its training, two weeks earlier—*"Five whole gallons of flaming gas!"* Through some diabolical means, the communists at Michelin had learned of the Operation although it was classified SECRET.

M, in its pleasant helicopters, would have a few tricks itself, mainly a new black nasty-looking rifle with a bullet that was a real terror, it tumbled end over end when it hit somebody. Sunday afternoon, Demirgian's squad sergeant had held one between his thumb and index finger, gazing at it long and philosophically—Hamlet, in some unwritten scene, contemplating his bare bodkin. "This . . ." the sergeant soliloquized as Demirgian sat listening, "this but a small little old job here. But it bring nothing but death," turning it with his thumb, thinking, *a real sensible bullet,* thinking of the skinny blue-tick hound that his uncle in Louisiana dog-hunted with: a real sensible hound, his uncle would say, whenever it treed a raccoon it would circle round the trunk, the coon couldn't escape. "This job," the sergeant continued, "it might make two or three circles in you 'fore it comes out. Hit you in the 'tomach, liable to come out the top of you' head. Charlie now, he'll do anything to get this weapon. He'll risk one hundred men jus' to get one of these weapons."

Well. That is just peachy-keeno, Demirgian had thought, though he also caught himself thinking, *yeah? Let him just try.* Demirgian's whole wild imagination had never foreseen a sergeant quite like his. The man was a Negro, short, with a chest like a sousaphone. In his teeth, which had gold veneer, with little hearts and stars of enamel flirtatiously peeking through, he was always clenching half a cigar, Demirgian had never seen his sergeant with one whole virgin cigar. Besides his drooping black mustache he had a tuft of scruffy Hassidic hair on one cheek, *keep it—it's lucky,* his grandma had pleaded when he was three, and though other kids had called him Fuzzy-face and Army officers blanched, Demirgian's fabulous sergeant wouldn't shave it away. His real name was Gore—Sergeant Gore.

"Okay," he had told Demirgian's squad the afternoon before the Operation. "What this is suppose' be about is getting off the 'copter. Run five meters and drop, because we don' want nobody getting hit by the 'peller. Get out and 'sperse. The first five minutes you can't hear nothing 'cept pop! pop! pop! flying over you' head. If anybody hit, just don' get panic' and jump up because then you'll get hit worser. Just yell medic. Just be cool, cool as you can, cool and calm, don' get shook up and crack up, just be cool," Sullivan biting his nails, Demirgian with eight yellow straws in his fingers intently weaving a place mat. "O...

...y become a PFC.
...find myself another kind of stripes,
because those yellow stripes, Charlie see those he's
goin' say, *I'm goin' get me a buck sergeant.* But when
we come back we got sewing to do. . . ."

. . . The trees became larger, the brown ground
was closer, slowly M's helicopters were coming
down. Even without its black rifles M had a real bag-
gage problem: everyone wore ammunition pouches,
two canteens, a shovel to make foxholes with, a gas
mask, a pack—on his pack suspenders, like bouton-
nieres, he had hand grenades, while each of the veterans had cigarettes or toilet tissues under a strap on
his steel helmet, where they wouldn't get soggy
crossing the streams. Yoshioka, by act of God an
assistant machine gunner, had three incredible
links of bullets pendulating from his neck to his
kneecaps, he looked like Wonga the king of Tonga in
his boar's-tooth beads. Demirgian had an outstanding canteen cup: he had been issued it after a week of
his drinking coffee from a pan, where it had sloshed
around like a strange dark lunar sea—he didn't
know it was collapsible, though, and he'd hung the
cumbersome thing over his belt buckle at a mendi-
cant angle, give to the Salvation Army. In his
backpack Demirgian had a can of Old Spice Shaving Cream. Sullivan had Rise mentholated and
Macleans Toothpaste. Neither of these infantrymen
had Jade East or Brut. Morton had Palmolive and
"Get down!" said Sergeant Gore. The helicopters

took off again and Demirgian found himself lying on a patch of hard dry dirt in a flat brown field. *Click—clack*—and Demirgian put a bullet into his rifle, the first bullet there since he came to Vietnam, *weapons are to be kept unloaded* was a standing order on the rubber plantation, the reason was so American boys wouldn't kill themselves. *Well,* Demirgian thought, *I guess this is a rice paddy,* the first he had ever observed—anyhow, it was surely no rubber plantation. Ha ha! the whole secret Operation order had been a trick, it was only a subterfuge, the soldiers, the Vietnamese army, everyone had been taken in, Smoke himself hadn't been set straight till the evening before. M wasn't anywhere near the Michelin funland, in keeping with a truly secret order it was twelve merciful miles to the south, hooray for the American army!

"Damn! Damn! Damn! I've lost a platoon," Demirgian's normally jolly captain was hurrying by and muttering, but he meant that he had misplaced it, nothing dire. If truth be told, the communists were so surprised by the Operation's popping out of the floor like a Punch and Judy puppet in this unadvertised place—so taken by surprise they weren't even there, and Demirgian had nobody to shoot at; nobody did. Sunshine shone. Barn swallows darted about. Really the invasion area was quite picnicky: a big warm waffle, a lot of dry paddies lying in a square grid of grassy dikes, one or two feet high. Demirgian was sitting at the angle where two of the dikes crossed and thinking, *so . . . ? when do we do something?* Destiny's abandoned child, he happened to be where abscissa and ordinate intersected, where $x = 0$ and $y = 0$ and all the forces and fortunes of war canceled out to just about nothing. On all sides of Demirgian, including up, episodes of some interest seemed to be entering history's pages, but coming between them and Demirgian was a consistent half a

"That son of a bitch," Smoke replied. "He has his head up his ass and locked," turning to his left and telling his pilot, Fu Manchu, to keep circling—well, the helicopter pilot certainly *looked* like Fu, his head was shaved bald, his black mustache hung to below his chin. He was a warrant officer.

Half a mile back of Demirgian's tranquil oasis, the battalion's operations officer was sitting on a C-ration carton spinning the knobs of his radio to inquire about some horrifying noises that carried across the sizzling paddies from the cavalry troop half a mile to Demirgian's right. At last the officer radioed to Smoke, half a mile above Demirgian, "All that activity apparently is recon by fire," meaning that the wags in the cavalry had apparently ridden to some astonished Vietnamese village on their steel horses and were firing into it with 50-caliber machine guns, the bullets as big as hot dogs, great big Oldenburg pop-art bullets, this being the cavalry's rip-roaring way of ascertaining if any communists resided there—if so, they'd doubtless return fire. With prudence, the other householders would have already toddled away. Half a mile to Demirgian's left, in a village whose ten or a dozen skedaddled families had been succeeded by Morton's company, Bigalow, wearing a black-and-white PIO on his arm, public information office, was sitting beneath a shady poncho having lunch with a girl whose lovely combat helmet wore a nest of red bougainvillea blossoms. Bigalow offered her some C-rations.

"No thanks, I'm not having any," the girl replied prettily, not wishing to eat until the cool of the afternoon—the temperature was in the 100s.

"Uh . . . where do you live?" Bigalow asked her.

"I've a little villa in Saigon," she answered, giving him a sisterly smile. She said her name was Beverly Deepe of the *New York Herald Tribune.*

Not far away, Morton was burning down Vietnamese houses, having been asked to. *"Stop burning all those houses!"* Smoke yelled into his radio, hitting the ceiling (the plexiglass, rather) half a mile above Demirgian's helmet. Fu was still flying him clockwise, his motionless hand on the cyclic stick, his whiskers becoming frowzy in the breeze and his thoughts going, *ugh! I'll have to paste 'em down with Mexican mustache wax tonight,* well, it was better than gasoline-resistant helicopter grease, which he had used for four months. "Stop burning down those houses!" Smoke told his captains by radio. "There's no VC in those houses!" The captains told their lieutenants don't burn the houses if there's no VC in them—the lieutenants told their sergeants if you burn those houses there had better be VC in them—the sergeants told their men go and burn those houses, there may be VC in them—and Morton kept striking his C-ration matches. Or something or other—anyhow, soon there wasn't a Vietnamese farmhouse that wasn't a layer of smoldering black dust.

Bored old Demirgian was still waiting on orders. Half a mile in front of him, something extraordinary happened in Williams's company, there was a gunshot! Bang! and a boy named Higdon started to bleed. "Sergeant, I've shot myself," Higdon said to his squad leader—he was truly embarrassed.

"What have you did?" the sergeant cried, but

on board and a correspondent for *Stars and Stripes* interviewed the operations officer.

"A sniper?"

"Well, a bullet."

Seconds later, thirty degrees cooler, his bleeding stanched, pale Higdon was being lifted to the field hospital, and Higdon's mimeographed form was being sped to the dusty division camp. There the facts and figures bearing on his misadventure were brought into an air-conditioned Army trailer as dark as a refrigerator room and translated into neo-Babylonian cuneiform on a white IBM card, which then was sacrificed to the only IBM accounting machine in any of this planet's combat areas, the newest pride of Major Sajo. A wan custodian tapping the icy-blue START button, the IBM machine began to whirr, chewing up twenty-five casualties every ten seconds and typing a current catalog of their curricula vitae in alphabetical order on paper as wide as piano rolls. Higdon's cool little card was just one second away from the IBM machine's teeth as *whirr*, the machine typed,

HICKMAN DALLAS E SGT

followed by a bleak row of code numbers whose tale was that Hickman had been slightly wounded, that he was single and lived in Ohio. Then, Higdon's card was one-half second away as *whirr* went the frigid machine, typing,

HICKMAN DALLAS E SGT

this version of Hickman's misfortune insisting that he had been killed, that he was married and lived in the hills of West Virginia. *Whirr,* went the IBM machine, above it a chilly little sign, "Talk about confusion! Did ya' ever have one of those crazy days when everything goes right?" *Whirr,* and it swallowed Higdon in one frosty bite.

HIGDON FRED F JR PFC

it typed, with a row of shivering numbers to say that Higdon was wounded in an area other than his head, torso, arms, or legs (it was Higdon's foot). Then the air-conditioned machine typed WHA, meaning that he had been *wounded—hostile action,* and even before the mighty Operation ended, Higdon, still in his hospital, his other foot wrapped in white bandages, was awarded the purple heart by the direction of President Johnson.

And! And there sat Demirgian at the dead center of this campaign, the calm eye of that whirlwind, the omphalos of all events, cleaning his fingernails. If anything, Demirgian felt a bit foolish—from where he sat, every disparity between this Operation and another dull training exercise was adventitious, the principal shade of difference was that it wasn't snowing. Reaching between his scratchy combat shirt and his T-shirt, Demirgian pulled out Saturday's *Stars and Stripes,* and sitting back against his dikes he read,

American losses were called "very light" despite the heavy machine gun and mortar fire.

"I believe it is now too late for disagreement as to whether we should be in South Vietnam," Stennis said in a Senate speech.

Demirgian read,

Conceding it was understandable that many Americans found the Vietnamese situation confusing, Rusk said . . .

Demirgian read,

Dagwood, guess what—Pauline is going to marry Richard.

Demirgian read,

But in common decency, widder—yo' oughta mourn yore husbin fo' at *least* a week!! Yo'd give a dog that courtesy!! A *roach!!*

Then, into the midst of his current-events class came Sergeant Gore. "Let's move," he said, and Demirgian got to his tingling feet as he told himself, *there's the Army, hurry up and wait!* Demirgian moved a mile and he dug himself a foxhole—all this was Monday.

Tuesday, Demirgian lay under his rubber poncho outside of his ragged foxhole, listening to two friends gripe. "Damn," said a specialist-four, a boy whose modernistic rank was equal to corporal, "we've got to sew those stripes on once we're back."

"And," said a sergeant, "we're not allowed to *sew* them, we've got to stich them."

"What do you mean, what's the difference?"

"Well, sew is by hand. Stitch is by machine."

"What do you mean, where do we get machines?"

"We don't, that's the *thing*. We've got to stitch them by hand. . . ."

That same Tuesday, Sullivan was assigned to KP, serving a bird colonel medium-rare roast beef and pouring him grapefruit juice—and that was Tuesday.

Wednesday, Demirgian walked into an ambush. *No! No one in this battalion ever is ambushed,* it had been shown syllogistically by Colonel Smoke! One: an ambush is unexpected—two: in this battalion we expect anything—three: so Q.E.D. it stands to reason that no one in this battalion is ever ambushed! Still, when one fierce communist company opened up on Demirgian with rifles, carbines, machine guns, recoilless rifles, grenades, and rifle grenades from behind some evergreen trees and people commenced bleeding and dying all about him, Demirgian was— may we say surprised? Surprised, then. Demirgian had started that day by shaving, brushing his teeth in his GI canteen water, and climbing aboard an APC: in combat, an APC being scarcely what it was in training, in the United States. There it was a pill, an aspirin-phenacetin-

...his wish to dance with Hawaii's lulu girls, he had thrown himself from an Army airplane the very morning that the Operation began, Scotty having gone to Georgia to become a paratrooper instead of a straight-leg soldier in the Far East.

No, an APC wasn't a pill but an armored personnel carrier, a crazy tanklike truck that the cavalry used to carry infantrymen over the paddies. Demirgian's idle platoon, six of it from M, had been attached to the cavalry this Wednesday morning, and standing in these fabulous steel Conestoga wagons it had driven east to a jungle that the playful cavalrymen knew as Sherwood forest, the same evergreen woodland where Charlie's rifle company lay in ambush, as dumb coincidence would have it. The temperature was in the 100s and clouds were few, the water on some of the paddies daintily reflecting them, a Fragonard effect. Once as their APCs passed some yellow Vietnamese houses where a sniper or two mightn't inconceivably lurk, the prudent cavalrymen paused and burned the pathetic little hamlet down, an act that any American whose heart goes out to the homeless will censure with a vehemence that is proportional to his range from the houses in question. Demirgian joined in with gusto, throwing his hand grenades into the thatch. Far from seeing this as senseless, Demirgian's inevitable point of view was—*finally!* finally he could do something with a clear bearing on America's war effort, clear in a physical sense if hazy around the edges in the sense of grand strategy. Now, Demirgian might be a wolf on the fold but a mickey-mouser, that he joyfully wasn't, and having done his patriotic duties he read a copy of *Stars and Stripes* as the APC rolled on. Demirgian's chariot had a steel skin and black rubber tractor treads as tough as an old bull elephant's foot, yellow straw in the tiny cracks. Its scowling driver sat amid steel and watched the paddies through what do you know? a periscope, and a brawny cavalry sergeant with a talcum of brown dust on his cheeks stood at the Oldenburg machine gun, two burly hands on its wooden handles, thumbs on its trigger. Coming near Sherwood forest, the cavalrymen told Demirgian to climb down and to walk ahead of the APC to protect it.

Walking with his platoon towards the opaque forest, the APCs snug as a bug in a rug behind him, Demirgian was reminded of the poem by Robert Frost, *Two roads diverged in a wood, and I—I took the one less traveled by,* good infantry tactics, that. Credit a little white puppy with saving Demirgian's life. Frightened by this rowdy cavalry column, it ran from behind a haystack and along the evergreens, hippity-hop on its spindly legs, the sergeant who didn't look forward to stitching shouting, "Hey! Look at that damn dog!" and Demirgian's whole teenaged platoon opening fire, everything it had. *Bang,* in a leg, then leaping, landing, stumbling along on its other three, with a *bang bang bang* the doggie died. Having been reared in poor villages where to waste meant to want, the communist troops in the underbrush couldn't conceive of a land so lavishly endowed that it had treasure to spare against man's best friend. Assuming this mighty barrage was meant for themselves, the communists began to return fire before Demirgian had walked over the last little paddy-dike into their killing zone. When the

... postal clerks. The mailmen had been authorized to shoot up to five blank bullets apiece, and when their little *pop . . . pop . . . pop . . . pop . . . pop* began to be heard from the snowy ponderosa pines, Demirgian's sergeant had promptly cried, "Three o'clock!" While not so stirring as "Up, soldiers, and at them" or *"Allons, enfants de la patrie,"* the horological order had a comparable effect and Demirgian's unit had turned to its right (to where it says "3" on clocks) and had plunged into the cold ponderosa shouting *aargh,* the letter carriers throwing up their shivering hands in mock surrender. The way the Army systematized it, a sergeant who believed in the creed of "He who fights and runs away—lives to fight another day" was allowed to cry, "Nine o'clock," in this tactical predicament, his unit turning its tail to the enemy and fleeing discreetly off to the left. Demirgian had been asked about this Army doctrine on his final exam, *a good way to break contact with the enemy is (a) the clock system, (b) mortars and artillery, (c) tear gas, or (d) leaps and bounds,* and though he had checked the right multiple choice—*(a) the clock system*—this morning in Vietnam he was learning that experience writes a textbook all its own. Caught in a real actual communist ambush, the rest of Demirgian's platoon had unanimously chosen a fifth alternative, *(e)* lying down on the ground behind the last paddy dike.

Demirgian had never seen honest-to-God communists until now—in fact he still didn't, peer as he might into the dense woods, the source of that infernal slapping racket. *"Get your ass down,"* the stitching sergeant screamed to him, and Sullivan, lying behind the dike and thinking, not at all frenziedly, *will I see Pam again?* or Debbie, for that matter, thinking detachedly and tugging on Demirgian's gas-mask bag, insistently tried to bring Demirgian to earth, but sturdy Demirgian kept standing there amid the *slap!* the horsewhip sounds like Washington crossing the Delaware, curious and desirous to see some flesh in that jungle to fire his black rifle at. Some soldiers Demirgian knew seemed to be dead already: a medic was dead, another friend was mortally wounded, neither had been in M company. The cavalry lieutenant was lying down, a bullet that the ghostly communists had aimed at his chest having struck his Star of David with the force of a battering ram. Another of those enemy poltergeists sent a bullet through a sergeant's helmet with an ear-shattering *ping . . . g,* in here, out there, the helmet ripping apart like a wet paper bag, the bullet missing the sergeant's head, strangely enough.

Slap! Slap! Slap! like a violent bit of applause or a vicious swipe at an insect. Demirgian aside, M was on its stomachs back of the knee-high dikes: out of the fire and into the frying pan, as it were. But here in M's grassy asylum, the celebrated effects of a baptism of fire, a cold sweat, a heart like a kettledrum, an unreliable sphincter, a shrinking-in of the nerves like a jellyfish pulling up its tentacles—the legendary symptoms were all surprisingly mild. The truth is that M had never quite had the imagination to see itself dead, a deficit of imagery that one more month in Vietnam was to partially redress. Demirgian's surplus of imagination came to the same thing, and amid these dangerous slapping sounds it carried him beyond fears of dying to fantasies of wondrously sur-

... heart and he
... A soldier crawled to him crying, *"Hey Doc!"* but
that soldier was shot as well. By now Demirgian saw
how valor and discretion needn't be incompatible,
and he was down behind his dike, a good soldier
obeying orders who *still* hadn't seen a communist.
From time to time he raised himself to peer or to fire
his rifle with a hopeful bang! into the forest—at
what, Demirgian kneweth not.

In this way, Demirgian came to appreciate the ee-
rie nature of his generation's war. On many, *most* of
the veterans in Vietnam, one will discern an uneasy
flitting of the eyes or an irresolute twitch at the corners of the mouth, it testifies how they've been a
year in the field boxing shadows, taking up arms
against a sea of unseen essences, locked in combat
with an insubstantial Kafkan vapor—that battle to
the death, an act whose only redeeming virtue had
been to make ordinary Roman men into heroes, now
makes American boys bewildered little Wozzecks instead. When silver airplanes started to dive-bomb
the trees, Demirgian could only lie behind his dike
and idly observe a colony of black termites eating a
gray beetle. Taking his insect repellent from his
pants pocket, Demirgian directed a fine needle spray
at one of these conspicuous enemies of man, a termite who stopped in the midst of its verminous meal
to look at Demirgian bug-eyed. Its shower bath continuing, the termite turned and fled to Demirgian's
right, oblivious of the super sabres that now dove in

from there to drop their bombs with a spherical *boom* on the terrified evergreen trees. "You dumb bunny," Demirgian said to his termite, "you're trying to get away from the stuff and it's all over you," the dizzy little pismire at last giving way to panic and falling over a precipice two inches high, out of its misery. Boom! As the silver bombers kept giving the vegetable kingdom a ruthless beating, a curious gray-green caterpillar happened along, and Demirgian squashed it with a twig while he said to that aborted butterfly, "Well—survival of the fittest and you're not fit." Boom! Boom! Boom! Well behind Demirgian, a Vietnamese in black pajamas ran from a haystack in panic, his arms in the skies to signal *I surrender,* and when an enraged cavalryman with a steel machete tried to wreak his vengeance on this anthropomorphous raw material a more self-collected boy rescued him. Taken prisoner, the Vietnamese was found to be nothing more nefarious than a scared farmer of sixty-four reverend years. His name is Nguyen Van Mang.

By now Charlie's spooky rifle company had spirited itself away, the first mellow *boom* of the dive bombers apparently being the cock's crow. Demirgian's unique Negro sergeant rose to his feet saying, "Let's get back to the 'PC," and after that, Wednesday had no worse sounds to offer M than a single hoarse but hyperbolic scream, *"I'm wounded!"* It rose from a boy whose neolithic jaw, a counterweight for an unseen bascule bridge, had kept his mouth irremediably open as he raced to the APC and tripped on a paddy-dike, biting his lip.

"Is it bleeding?" he cried as M rode bumpily and blissfully back to its foxholes, Sullivan eating a C-ration fruitcake, Demirgian doing the puzzle page in the Junction City *Union. "Nya-a!"* showing them his uninteresting wound.

That night in their welcome holes, the hard-bitten

Thursday, Williams, the gentle Florida periscope operator, achieved immortality of sorts: he
really saw a communist, large as life and twice as
spunky, an experience that no other trooper in M's
alert battalion was to enjoy throughout this Operation. This special communist was staring at Williams from a bush no farther than the other side of a
ping-pong table, staring at him down the gray barrel
of a rifle, in fact. *"Ho!"* Williams shouted in consternation: but to begin at the beginning.

On Thursday, Demirgian's deserving platoon took
a siesta as Williams's company and Morton's company walked through the dark of Sherwood forest,
slow going, all sorts of tangly things, little red ants,
the mission being to destroy the source of Charlie's
strength: the communist stores of rice. Every time
Williams's snail-paced friends came to one they
burned it—two or three tons of this brown, riverlike
stuff could keep Charlie's battalion marching on its
stomach a week, the idea being. A gay little Vietnamese soldier went along to sanction any or all burn-
ings or blowings up, first having satisfied himself
that the rice was truly communist, the soldier having been trained in this mystic art. Once as machetes
cut through the bushes, Williams's company came to
a stock of Vermont-like maple candy in laundry-soap
sized bars. But being in a cave it just wouldn't burn.
An inventive sergeant began to throw the sugary

stuff to the ants—but no, too time-consuming. Hand grenades? Now he had maple candy with holes. Nausea-inducing gas? Nothing doing, it might be against the Geneva Convention. At last the patient sergeant radioed the Army engineers, who blew up the maple candy with TNT. Bigalow was on this safari in his flack capacity, *a story!* he told himself but he couldn't write it, a public information sergeant having told him it wouldn't pass Army censorship. "You're not winning friends among Vietnamese farmers," Bigalow's sergeant had explained.

Even with machetes, moving in this jungle was like searching in a big attic closet on a summer morning, old moist bathrobes drawing across one's face and rusty old clothes hangers snagging in one's hair, corrugated cardboard beneath one's feet. Furthermore, in this wildwood there were snipers shooting at people, a rustling in the leaves and a *slap!* But what really bedeviled Williams's and Morton's companies as they pushed along weren't their human enemies but ants, little red ants which hadn't seen juicy Westerners in a quarter century, even the French army hadn't dared go to this treacherous place. Morton would tell himself, *Oh—! here comes another one,* as still another cackling ant threw itself out of the foliage onto his neck, and Morton would roll it off with sweating fingers, his black rifle in his other hand, pressing it to instant death. Morton felt guilty about his extraordinary acts of self-assertiveness; a Baptist, he didn't think God set anything on this earth without having His reason, maybe in little red ants was a liquid to cure malaria, cancer, doctors would find it some day, Morton piously believed. For weeks he would justify his steady slaughter by telling himself, *it didn't make any difference—there were so many of them.* He would remonstrate with Russo, the young desperado of sixteen who swore that if *he* had been in those

...jungle floor. But as Bigalow inched along he also speculated whether there wasn't a story in them, *How to Kill Ants, by PFC Vaughan A. Bigalow.* He thought, *One way is to throttle your ant by pushing a grain of sand into its throat with a toothpick. A second way* . . . a microscopic punji pit, a careless ant expiring horribly on the point of a pin. In practice Bigalow killed his ants conventionally: indifferently, paying no mind to their dying agonies while he walked along with the friend who once had twitted him about his ball-point pen, I stabbed! I stabbed! I stabbed! "Bigalow," the boy remembered in this incongruous place, "tell Dubitsky he owes me five dollars."

"All right," said Bigalow, slapping a neck-ant.

"And Bigalow. You've got a pair of my khakis."

"You're right," said Bigalow, dropping his dead ant down.

"And Bigalow? If the captain doesn't get us out of here, you can have the other pair, too."

But Williams—! It never occurred to Williams's gentle mind to kill these ants: if one of them bit he just brushed it off without taking his grim revenge. And that was Williams's nonbelligerent temper when he had that sudden brush with his communist, a Vietnamese with a white shirt and *hair*—black hair, Williams would never forget his bushy hair. Resting in a little jungle hole, a gully, hearing a twig crack, turning around, Williams saw this black-haired intruder and shouted, *"Ho,"* ducking into his hole. A bullet burned across his shoulder blade and Williams cried out, *"Oh,"* burying his startled face in the dirt, holding his rifle high above him like an African's spear, shooting it at the trees one-handed, bang! bang! bang! and crying, *"Sergeant! sergeant! sergeant! come here!"* My kingdom for a periscope!

"What's the matter?" Williams's sergeant called as he hurried to this clamorous scene.

"Keep shooting!" Williams shouted while he did exactly that, his face still plowing into the dirt. *"I seed one!"*

"Where?"

"Out there! He shot me," jerking his head up, spying the evergreen trees but no more communist.

"Whereabouts?"

"Here—in the shoulder!"

"Nothing. Maybe a ricochet breezed across it."

"Sergeant, that was no ricochet! I'm hit, I know I'm hit!"

"Rock steady!" said Williams's unruffled sergeant. "You aren't hit, you've nothing to worry about, you're okay. Rock steady."

Williams got dazedly to his feet and stared around. He told his sergeant, "Okay, I'll try."

"Can you make it through the jungle?"

"I'll try."

But as Williams resumed his death-march through the tangled vines, the tendrils plucking at his shoulders, pulling at his feet, he feared to see that black-haired man staring at him from every bush, he imagined the vines to be black hair, black hair to condense from the shadowy air. Red ants fell on Williams's sleeve, and Williams dully brushed them off. *I get through this I'm never going back—never!*

His black-haired nemesis or someone else was shooting Americans all of their arduous way through the forest, *slap!* and *slap!* killing two of

—g, when a sergeant said, *"You're a real good goddam soldier,"* he only laughed. Somebody lit a lighter, *"The lieutenant doesn't want you to,"* *"Fuck the lieutenant,"* the house was in black-tongued flames. Somebody used a grenade launcher, there was nothing left.

The following calm morning, Williams went to his sergeant's foxhole to talk to his sergeant and to declare himself *hors de combat.* A young-looking boy from the East, Williams's sergeant had earned his reputation for infinite patience as leader of the bowl patrol back on M's cool rubber plantation. Next to each rubber tree was a sort of white cereal bowl, in late afternoon the Vietnamese tree-tappers left it rightside-up to gather rubber or upside-down if it threatened rain. But going above and beyond the call of duty, the Vietnamese had also put certain bowls in a third—unauthorized—attitude: tilted, the rubber sap in the moonlight showing the communist snipers which way to shoot to kill American soldiers best. Evening after evening, Williams's patient sergeant had taken his bowl patrol into the shadowy trees to tilt the white bowls back to the proper horticultural angle. Williams could have no more compassionate audience than the saint he was telling today, "Now, I don't want you to think I'm a comprehentious objector."

"Do you mean a com— conscientious objective?"

"I don't want you to think I'm one of those. I'll do

anything you want me to: exceptin' to kill somebody."

"Well," said Williams's sergeant gently. "Don't you think you're giving up too easy?"

"No, serge, I've tried, I've tried, I've made up my mind. I haven't got it in me to kill, I found that yesterday."

"Well, there ain't none of us wants to kill someone. But if it's something got to be done, somebody's got to do it, that's all."

"Serge, I'm just no use in the jungle unlessin' I can kill someone. I ain't going back in the jungle—I just ain't going back."

"Well, *somebody* got to go back in that jungle, Charlie ain't coming out," Williams's patient sergeant concluded.

In the weeks after that at M's sylvan rubber plantation, the soft light slipping through the tall trees, the birds in the leaves, a monkey—the weeks after that, Williams's sergeant made sweet remonstrances, Williams's first sergeant made terrible threats, a court-martial, six years at hard labor, a dishonorable discharge, but neither the stick nor carrot could change Williams's simple belief, kill or be killed was the law of that jungle and he wanted neither. "The spunkless wonder," his bitter lieutenant called him at the officers mess, thinking, *he's selfish, he's unpatriotic, he says he's scared—well, so everyone's scared,* and Williams's captain remembered his Goethe class at college, *he only earns his freedom and existence who daily conquers them anew.* Amen to that, the other diners would say, telling themselves *there's a war on but Williams won't do his part!* The officers had learned to tolerate this in the Vietnamese army, but Williams—he was an American!

An ambulance having been called for, Williams was taken to the rubber plantation's bright landing

liams replied.

"Now how did this come about?" Distantly the psychiatrist was thinking, *autism—association—ambivalence—affect,* the four signs of schizophrenia they had taught him at Colorado. One of those telltale *a*'s—well, we're none of us perfect. Two of them, uh-oh, three of them, *zap!* a medical discharge for poor old psychotic Williams.

Williams sat in a chair by the doctor's little desk, the same catty-corner furniture arrangement at which he had once sought work at the VC, the Virginia Carolina Mining Corporation, $1.97 an hour. All that Williams knew of psychiatrists he had acquired on television: he believed that his red-headed doctor would give him some bright-colored blocks to put together in two minutes, schizophrenia he hadn't heard of, three of those *a*'s would be gibberish to Williams, *association* might mean the Knights of Pythias or the NAACP, neither of which he had joined. In all innocence he sat in that sweltering tent and answered the doctor's friendly questions. Williams's father had drowned. Williams had had headaches for a month after that. He lived with his mother, but he had a girl. Kathernell was her name. Williams wanted to marry her, and some day he would. Ten minutes later the doctor wrote, *"No illness found,"* on Williams's mimeographed form and sent him back to his rifle company, where the captain made him a cook instead of a combat soldier and where he learned to mix water, flour, lard, and dark brown gravy base to make gravy.

But back to Friday of the Operation.

Friday the long awaited happened—M's battalion killed somebody, at last. "What's the spirit of the bayonet?" those wild-eyed sergeants had cried to M in America. *"To kill!"* M had learned to shout fiercely back. "The enemy is dedicated—he won't scare away," old Smoke, its battalion commander, had said to M, eyes aflame. *"You've got to kill him."* And on Friday morning M inevitably killed, doing its climactic job with mixed feelings, one understands, some of its soldiers queasy in the presence of waxy death, some of them impassive. M had guessed it would be this way—in training camp, Hofelder pictured a communist running at him savagely, he had asked himself, *could I really kill him?* but a buddy of his simply laughed, saying, "Shucks. I'm me and he's he," meaning that if I kill a fellow that is his worry, not mine.

The episode was the doing of Demirgian's platoon, again it had climbed on those hot APCs and had driven *bump —bounce —bump* to Sherwood forest and beyond, burning more yellow houses as it went. In actual fact, the cavalry's big lieutenant colonel had given the order, *insure that positive identification be made:* a sniper in the house destroy it, otherwise spare it. But through the iteration of imperatives and the abolition of qualifiers and a wise apprehension that the colonel couldn't be serious, his order was almost unrecognizable when it got through channels to Demirgian's Sergeant Gore. Gore heard the order as, "Kill everything. Destroy everything. Kill the cows, the pigs, the chickens—everything."

"Well, sir. You can't destroy *everything*," Gore

M

cavalrymen and De-
mirgian's platoon had been traveling since 7—*weird*,
Sullivan thought as the morning got hotter, observing that his steel vehicle was always in sunshine,
never in shade, although there were scores of white
sheep-clouds in the blue above him: a meteorological
mystery. But the wonder of wonders was Demirgian.
An unaccustomed competence seemed to have stolen
across Demirgian's features: his eyes level, his rifle
at a steady angle of attack, he reminded one of that
paragon of infantrymen that had been painted like a
rampant lion on each of their training camp's objets
d'art, even on the insides of teacups at the officers'
mess. Wednesday had satisfied Demirgian's romantic heart, it had confirmed Demirgian's faith: if he
didn't stand in lines but stayed in cavalry columns, if
he didn't shoulder a rifle to salute with but to shoot
with, ah—then the American army needn't be closed
to life's grander moments. Getting into the spirit of
his fierce orders, Demirgian shot at a water buffalo
and heartily he fired tracers into the yellow hay-
stacks to kindle them. Newman, M's philosophical
alligator trapper, a boy to whom the essences of old
country stores, of apple barrels and mackinaws,
adhered—Newman climbed from his APC to set fire
to one yellow farmhouse, but since he had seen
women and children running from it one minute
earlier he had serious doubts about the propriety
of his task. He said to his sergeant, "Now, why
should I do this? They'll just build another tomor-

row," but really he was thinking, *I burn their farmhouse down, that'll just make them communists, won't it,* Smoke himself had asserted so. Still, Newman obeyed his orders, using his Army matches, closing the cover before striking them, the cover inscribed, "Where liberty is, there is my home—Benjamin Franklin," the apocalypse drove on.

Then it was that the incident happened. A cavalry sergeant, seeing a sort of bunker place, a hut above, hole below, and hearing some voices inside it, told Demirgian to throw a grenade in. Demirgian hesitating, ——, a soldier we have met before, though not by name, jumped from his APC and flipped in a hand grenade himself. It rolled through the door hitting a sort of earthen baffle before it exploded, and —— gasped as ten or a dozen women and children came shrieking out in their crinkled pajamas: no blood, no apparent injuries, though, and —— got onto his carrier again, it continued on. The next APC in the column, with Yoshioka aboard, drove up to this hovel, and a Negro specialist-four, his black rifle in his hands, warily extended his head in, peering through the darkness one or two seconds before he cried, *"Oh my God!"*

"What's the matter," said a second specialist.

"They hit a little girl," and in his muscular arms the Negro specialist brought out a seven-year-old, long black hair and little earrings, staring eyes— *eyes,* her eyes are what froze themselves onto M's memory, it seemed there was no white to those eyes, nothing but black ellipses like black goldfish. The child's nose was bleeding—there was a hole in the back of her skull.

Needless to say, America hadn't sent M into battle without having taught it the principles of first aid. Sergeants had spun around like T-formation quarterbacks to slap hypothetical wounds into the torso,

pressure bandage, (*c*) press on a pressure point, and (*d*) apply a tourniquet—of course, a tourniquet wouldn't be indicated in the accident today. Nor could it be argued that M was all surgical competence with no human heart, not in the least. If its oral exams had proved anything, it was that M would try to be Nightingales as well as Galens whenever bleeding occurred, many of its tenderhearted boys reciting the Army's four iatrical measures and adding a fifth of their own, "I'd first make him *real* comfortable," or "I'd talk to him . . . I'd talk to him." Providence had placed the first of those compassionate soldiers at the door to this morning's bunker, but an injury as massive as that staring girl's went far beyond his earnest abilities, and even a PFC medic was saying sadly, "There's nothing to be done."

A cavalry sergeant pressed his thumb on the press-to-talk switch of his radio and reported to his captain, "Sir, there's a little girl, a civilian girl, who is wounded. Can we have a dust-off?" The sergeant hoped for a helicopter to bring the gazing child to one of Vietnam's civilian hospitals, where the patients lie three to a bed with weird afflictions like missing arms and legs and holes in parts of their bodies.

"Roger," said the cavalry captain, but then the seven-year-old shuddered and died.

"Sir," said the cavalry sergeant, "the little girl died."

"Roger," said the captain and the APCs moved on, pausing only for specialist number two to give the other children chewing gum and to comfort the girl's mother as best he could, "We're sorry," the mother shaking her head embarrassedly as though to say *please—it could happen to anyone,* a piece of shrapnel sticking out of her shoulder; the medic gave her a bandage before he left.

One doesn't doubt, in the many months to come M would see operations with a greater share of glory (and it would see many, the Army would need fifteen hundred operations as vast as this to cover all Charlie's territory, and Charlie might still be back the following evening)—more glorious operations, but this first Operation of M's had come to its melancholy close, and M's tired battalion was to kill, wound, or capture no other Vietnamese, communist or otherwise, estimated or actual, in the day-and-a-half remaining. Some of M was truly ashamed about the seven-year-old. Sullivan was annoyed with her, *dammit,* he thought, *she should have known we didn't want to hurt her. Why was she hiding out?* Much of M agreed with him, *ignorant people,* they thought. A cavalry lieutenant had no misgivings, thinking, *these people don't want us here anyhow, why should I care about them?* a thought that he bitterly volunteered in conversation. In his innocent past, the lieutenant had gone through the empty-looking villages without taking care to destroy them first, a man, a woman, a *boy* opening fire and killing those for whose lives he was responsible. Vietnam had shown to the lieutenant's satisfaction the line where compassion must end, caution begin.

Yoshioka had stood by the bunker watching the girl die. He felt no special affinity toward Asia's troubles, though he was Oriental and his mother had been at Hiroshima, but being an American he did like children—he turned away, his face waxily para-

hand out, reaching his hand, reaching his, reaching—
three Fridays later in the black explosion Yoshioka
was freakishly wounded the same way as that staring child. The sergeant who touched the trip-wire
was killed, the Negro who'd found the little girl
was killed, M's old alligator trapper, Newman, was
ripped in his arms and legs by the whistling pieces of
steel and evacuated, and "Yokasoka's dead," the soldiers were saying that night at their rubber plantation, still not getting his name right, not knowing
how Yoshioka lay in a Saigon hospital vegetally
alive, huge Frankenstein stitches on his shaven
head, his acne caked with blood, a hole in his throat
to breathe through, bubbles between his lips, the
soles of his feet a queer pale yellow, his head thrash-
ing right and left as though to cry *no-no-no,* his hand
slapping his thigh as though he'd heard some madcap story, a sheet around the bedframe to hold him
in—a jar of clear liquid dripping into him, a
brownish-yellow liquid dripping out, a PFC shooing
the flies away and sucking things out of him with a
vacuum machine, a Navaho nurse pulling the sheet
up for modesty's sake, a doctor leaning over him
whispering, "Bob? You're in a hospital. You're going
to be on your litter a while. You're going to be traveling some. First you'll be on a plane. . . ."

It happened that the bed next to Yoshioka's was a
crib, inside it a stuffed red polka-dot puppy and a
wide-eyed Vietnamese girl of two. Tiny white plaster
casts like dinner candles kept her from picking her

moist upper lip, where Yoshioka's gentle and good-samaritan doctor had operated to correct a cleft, an ugly defect since her birth.

Saturday, the last scheduled day of the Operation and the fiftieth since the day when Milett had told M, "I got a wife, three kids at home . . . ," Saturday, M had nothing to do but push little squares of cotton through its rifle barrels. Demirgian said, "I cleaned it yesterday," and with a specialist-four he sat cross-legged on the grass by his foxhole doing the crossword puzzle in *Stars and Stripes*, his curved back to the communists, if any. "Appellation of Athena. That's a good one," Demirgian murmured.

"Room in a harem," the specialist countered softly.

"Ten down?" Demirgian.

"Nine down," the specialist.

"Ten down is girl's name is Ann."

"Nine down."

"Nine down is room in a harem."

"Like a bedroom?"

"Nine down is what?" Demirgian asked the elements.

Sullivan sat reading *The Unanswered Questions About President Kennedy's Assassination.* Russo was lying down: his beloved bowie knife had vanished in the woods like Excalibur in the lake, he had heat exhaustion besides, and under a coconut tree he whispered his secret age to his comrades in arms, hoping they might betray him to the authorities. Morton sat in his foxhole eating his C-rations, pleasantly asking his friends about why they burned down the Vietnamese houses—*he* felt funny about it. Friday morning Morton had asked a squad leader, "Sergeant, should I burn this house?" "Here, this'll

ter a few experiences of their trying to kill him. One of his friends said, "All these people, the VC take their brothers and fathers away, so if they've got family in the VC of course they'll be VC sympathizers." Another friend said, "Look at it this way. If you burn their house, if they're not a VC now they'll be one after you've burned their house," by which he meant go ahead and burn it, a tight little circle of reasoning that made even Morton blink. A third of his friends said simply, "I burn because I hate. I hate Vietnam. I hate it because I'm here. I hate every house, every tree, every pile of straw and when I see it I want to burn it." He seemed surprised to learn that the rest of Morton's friends had intellectual reasons, as well.

"Well," said Morton, laughing, "I guess in a few months I'll be burning houses too!" But that wasn't to happen. For walking down the road two weeks later, there was a noise and Morton died, the victim of one of Charlie's mines, his legs in the dusty dirt at raggedy-ann angles—Morton seemed to have three or four legs. "We held divine memorial services in his honor," the Chaplain wrote to Morton's mother and father in Texas. "Many were the generous tears as we reflected upon this profound truth, *Greater love hath no man than this, that a man lay down his life for his friends*. It may," the Chaplain wrote in his standard letter, "also be of comfort for you to remember that Billy was serving in a noble cause, helping good people to live in freedom here and all over the world. You remain in my prayers," the Chaplain wrote to Morton's parents, who buried him in his one-button suit.

"Site of Taj Mahal," the specialist-four was saying.

"India! India!" Demirgian cried.

"Too many letters," the specialist told him. Once they were through with the puzzle, they turned to the news and discovered a story on the Operation, several days old, on page one.

"Gee," Demirgian said, "I didn't think they'd write so much about *this.*"

"The division," the specialist said, reading out loud, *"was in the midst of its biggest campaign of the Vietnam war,* hey I didn't know that, *after pouring thousands of troops into a rugged wooded area . . ."*

"Wooded!" Sullivan looked up and cried.

"The battle-hardened division . . ."

"Battle-hardened! Ha!"

" . . . relying heavily on the element of surprise to catch a huge Vietcong force believed to be holing up in the district, launched its drive with lightning speed at daybreak Monday morning. Troops and tanks, along with armed personnel carriers, have swept into the area to close off the entire circle. Another force of troops is sweeping through the woods to the east. . . ."

"Caught in the crossfire!" Sullivan cried.

"Whenever the VC duck we shoot each *other,"* the specialist chortled.

And so M's merriment continued until a sergeant came marching to this perimeter to tell its defenders to quit goofing off, "Demirgian! Police up those papers—pick up those C-ration cans!" And out into no-man's land Demirgian walked, telling himself that the Army's the Army's the Army . . . but thinking it with a new-found equanimity and getting himself an old C-ration peanut butter lid, a C-ration chicken and noodles can, and an empty carton of

PFC, he had busted out of officer candidate school, *lack of mental adaptability,* and Mason had never become a green beret. A convert to candor, Russo was home in Yonkers with his honorable discharge. McCarthy was on leave in Islip seeing his lawyer and— *stop the presses!* He wasn't in Islip anymore, he was awol, he was over the hill, McCarthy at last was *wanted* by the military police—but Demirgian was still in Vietnam. Newman was on the rubber plantation driving a jeep, he was limping and couldn't fight, and Williams was in the kitchen making gravy and waiting— waiting— *why doesn't Kathernell write?* Bigalow had reenlisted till 1970, a bonus of $500. Some of M had medals, a third of M's expeditionary force had been killed or severely wounded, some of M had malaria, M, at times, had been accidentally napalmed or rocketed or shot in the head by its sergeants, a second wave of M was upon the waters, Hofedler with it: all aboard to South Vietnam! But Demirgian—

Demirgian was still in his fighting squad, the General chose it *best in battalion.* The infantryman *terrible,* terror of sergeants, had himself become an acting sergeant, the leader of five eager privates. While he still hadn't seen any communists, neither had he met a Vietnamese who cared a fig about communists or a feather about his fighting them. On operations, Demirgian shot at the pigeons and people's chickens, he stared at the high yellow flames, he found the American army good. Without any qualms he told his squad, *"I'd like to burn the whole country down and start again with Americans."* Half of Demirgian's tour of duty was safely over and done.

pen to fall, ninety-eight bottles of beer on the wall.
Ninety-eight. . . .

On the bottom side of earth in that strange land of
Vietnam, time is a row of old brown bottles that are
toppling down, of concrete balls that are cracking
apart—time, in Vietnam, is a great burlap bag of
rocks, and each day a soldier's shoulders are light-
ened of one more pound. As the night disappears, as
sun makes the metal mess kits shine and warms a
boy's cheeks, as day breaks he tells himself words like
"Ninety-nine days." The next day he tells himself,
"Ninety-eight. . . ."

Tonight is the last night of Demirgian's tour of
duty. Demirgian, a boy with the rank of specialist, his
specialty being the rifle, his duty being to kill communists with it—Demirgian, the three hundreds, two
hundreds, one hundreds over, the days strewn behind
him like little worthless pieces of broken glass, a stale-
ness issuing out of them, a sickening smell—Demirgian has just tonight left as a rifleman in Asia. And
when those seemingly endless hours are safely behind
him—hurrah! Demirgian comes marching home
again, uninjured, undead! Everybody cross your fingers! Pray for Demirgian! Pray!

That night Demirgian lay in his combat clothes—his steel helmet, the damp fabric of his shirt and trousers, his canvas boots—and Demirgian had a wet black rifle on the soil beside him as with intricate fingers he made himself grape juice. Slower than a caterpillar chews on a maple leaf his fingers tore a small paper packet of Kool-Aid and quieter than a dandelion loses its fluff his hand shook the light purple powder into his Army canteen. The cold stars above, the cool earth below him kept their complete silence as Demirgian tilted his rubber canteen to its left—right—left—right—with the slow periodicity of a pendulum. One long minute of this and Demirgian took a quiet sip. And ah! Demirgian came alive! He's in the grape-juice generation now! He buried the torn paper packet quietly in six inches of Vietnam's soil.

The time was ten or ten-thirty at night. It shouldn't be thought that on ambush parties (for Demirgian's invisible squad had an ambush assignment tonight: to lie in the total darkness, if anyone comes it's a communist, kill him)—it shouldn't be thought that on ambush parties the soldiers lie like panthers ready to leap, their legs up under them, their eyes all alert: ridiculous. The essence of American ambushes is that nothing—*nothing*—happens, nowhere but in the grave do the endless hours pass by a mass of human substance so stubbornly true to its configurations of one hour earlier, nobody in an American ambush party does a cotton-picking thing, the hours between sunset and sunrise hang as languidly as a hammock between two willow trees, one in a hundred times does a star-crossed communist happen by—a real event. Demirgian, a year of these uninteresting affairs and he still hadn't ambushed one living breath-

...ences of Asia hour

after hour and hi-di-ho, I should have brought my yo-yo, at dawn he had lifted himself like a heavy canvas tarpaulin and carried himself back to the company camp. It was three meals a day, pink pills on Sunday, payday on the thirtieth—it was a living, it soon would be over, America hello!

And so Demirgian lay in a last night of lassitude. Elsewhere in this ambush party a pair of flat shadows coalesced and imperceptible whispers rose. "Sergeant?"

"Yes?"

"Sergeant. I have a headache."

"You have a headache?"

"Sergeant? You have an aspirin?"

"Yes."

Another boy in Demirgian's dull ambush party quietly snored. The sergeant in charge of this tableau said his bedtime prayers, he said to himself, *"Padre nuestro,"* bowing his dark-colored face to the earth, *"que estas en los cielos. . . ."* The sergeant prayed for a typical night: no communists.

A VISIT TO THE BULLET FACTORY. *Splash! At the factory where the bright bullets for Demirgian's rifle are made, Connecticut citizens in big iron shoes are carrying lead to the melting pot—splash! From out of the press comes the hot wet wire, the width of a bul-*

*let's width, the length of eternity, and Curtis, a col-
ored man, a giant, the wire in his muscular hands,
his body bowed over the floor like an ogre's over a
steaming caldron, is coiling it—coiling it—oiling it,
the machinery sends it along. The machinery is gar-
gantuan, the gears are like wagon wheels, the con-
rods are making the motions of steady animal love.
And chop! And chop! The wire is cut into bullet sizes,
the slippery bullets slide from the chopping block on a
gangway of grease, they are slithering, skiddering,
and slippering into one another—sleighs on a snowy
hillside, jingle all the way!*

*Careful of the powdery stuff, boys and girls. Like
little chipped pieces of pencil lead, it comes to the bullet plant in cases, it gets itself on clothing like a city's
soot, it makes the wooden floor of the factory like a
ballroom floor, as though beneath the balls of the feet
lay little ball bearings. Roll out the barrel! To Agnes,
in her sensible shoes, the floor's like the floor of the
Pleasure Beach Ballroom, in Bridgeport. We'll have a
barrel of. . . . Agnes had met her husband there as
the polka played. With her cardboard card and a
brisk black brush, Agnes sweeps up the powder once
every day, as David with his—bang—with his little
leather—bang—with his little leather mallet—*BANG,
*David hits the feeder lines to clean them, too. No
smoking, please, as busy little birdlike ladies in
glasses of plastic take the black powder, the bullets,
the brass, as forty-nine at one time of these instrumen-
talities are made in the U.S.A. And a thousand
wheels go round and round! And the air's on edge in
the factory sound! And boxes of bullets abound on the
ground! And—*

*Click. Clack. Mechanically, Demirgian puts one of
Connecticut's bullets into his mean-looking rifle. A
power uncalled upon, a lion asleep, here in its cave the
bullet shall sit in steely silence all through an Asian
night, an unnecessary accessory to American ambush*

nist. And he has adequate reason. A year in the Vietnam bushes (the endless series of stops and starts, the waits at the ambush sites, the walks)—a year minus a day in Vietnam and Demirgian has still never seen a communist to shoot at. Typical.

The time was getting on past eleven. Demirgian lay on his hard lumpy mattress of earth—the ambush area, as across from him in the bushes a little thickening of blackness seemed to have suddenly moved, like a fish in the Stygian deep. Old soldier Demirgian tiredly recognized it for what it was, a banana leaf in the evening breeze. If only it were a communist soldier—ah! *Charlie tries to creep up on me,* Demirgian wistfully said to himself—*Charlie ever tries that and I'm just going to lie here—yeah! Let him get ten meters from me, the stupid little son-of-a. Yeah, and I'll have my hand grenade and I'll pull the pin—Charlie you're about to have had it! k-k-k! And then I'll let the handle go and I'll one—! two—! and I'll throw it!* Thumb on the bottom, fingers on top, a lazy little catlike windup, the pitch—Demirgian saw himself throw the grenade like a baseball, a rock, Demirgian had had some practice at that in Newton, Massachusetts, the city he had been drafted from and had been a schoolboy before. *"Foreigner,"* some of the other kids had cried at Demirgian, *"Camel*

chaser," some of the Irish would say, and Demirgian,
age twelve, his body behind a cardboard carton with
its color of dead lawns and a dry-spell smell, his eyes
at two tiny fiber-filled holes—Demirgian had thrown
lumps of pudding stone at the Irish children, that is
how he would throw his grenade at that communist
if the stars in their slowly maundering courses
should offer him—*at last*—one of his unseen enemies.
To kill a communist soldier: that was Demirgian's
dream, the Irish had been the object of nothing like
it, this was Demirgian's sacred quest. For a boy with
no past history of animus to Asians of any political
party, a year on that distant continent and Demirgian's wish to kill communists had gone beyond all
expectations, it was something fierce, his bones had
become like a thing turned black, a thin black liquid
ran in his arteries, no other friends of his felt it that
passionately, the reason—that was Demirgian's secret. A bullet, a piece of his bayonet, it didn't make a
diff to Demirgian *how,* a tent peg if it was sharp
enough, a shovel, a can of kerosene, a kitchen match
and—*bastard, die!* Demirgian's imagination knew
no mercy—kick him in the genitals, finger in his eyeballs, stick him in the ashcan, ha-ha-ha! *Yeah,* Demirgian thought in his wait at this ambush area, it
might be the night tonight—a toss of a hand grenade,
success! An explosion, *and I'll look at him lying there
dead and I'll think*—Demirgian thought of a pale yellow face, the mouth like a broken bottle, the starlight on crooked teeth—*I think I'll be sorry about
him—yeah,* Demirgian thought. *I'll say to him poor
bastard! You're fighting for a losing cause!* And later
if there was a watch upon him, Demirgian thought
he might take it, a souvenir.

It wouldn't be easy. The practical fact of Vietnam
is that the airplane pilots and artillerymen kill the
communists while riflemen like Demirgian kill
themselves—one doesn't have to say: by accident—

written—*our forearms [were being] slashed by thorns and our fatigues drenched with sweat. Suddenly*—suddenly a pal of Demirgian's had seen a real enemy soldier—*the bullet ripped through the Vietcong's head.* Though his name was spelled wrong in *Newsweek,* the commie-killing infantryman had been given a hero's due by Demirgian's proud battalion commander, a trip via cargo plane to the China Sea, a holiday spree at the beaches—time out, a Coppertone tan, a blanket, sand, a date in a blue bikini, only the brave deserve the fair! Another day, a Red was made dead by the steady machine gun of Demirgian's best friend—his buddy. His holiday over, Demirgian's friend had returned to the envious squad with his China Sea suntan to learn that he had been recommended for a medal—a bronze star and a "V" for valor—in addition, in recognition of that extraordinary act. It wasn't unheard of, Demirgian knew!

RECOMMENDED AWARD OF THE BRONZE STAR MEDAL. *"With complete disregard for his own personal safety and well-being ——— moved the machine gun to the forward position of the platoon and began placing accurate fire on enemy positions. His actions are in keeping with the highest traditions of the military service, and. . . ."*

Obligatory words. Kill every communist in China

*and still you'll get no medal to wear if your company
commander's letter of recommendation doesn't say
that you've done it with a certain very specific élan. It
is Army tradition—if a man's to receive a medal of
honor a letter of recommendation has to follow form
in saying verbatim, "He never relented from his determined effort to destroy the enemy," and Demirgian's
best friend is certain to be laughed out of court if the
letter in which he's recommended for a bronze star
and a "V" for valor leaves it unsaid that he killed his
communist in a way that evinced the virtues of aggressiveness, devotion to duty, and bravery, and if it
doesn't say, "His actions are in keeping with the highest traditions." All these amenities observed, the letter of recommendation has been given to a clerk with
the order to send it speedily through the Army's
channels—someone has killed a communist, hurrah!*

AWARD OF THE BRONZE STAR MEDAL. *"By direction of
the President, under the provisions of the executive order 11046, the Bronze Star Medal is awarded to
————— for outstanding meritorious service as a
company clerk in. . . ."*

*Fie on that clerk—he has thrown the letter of recom-
mendation away and given the Bronze Star to himself, the stinker! A very latent heterosexual, the clerk
has a way of walking in the company camp and
throwing his soft weight around as though he were
keeping a hula-hoop up—a typical Army clerk, and he
isn't about to let medals go to those awful-awful boys
in Demirgian's squad who always make fun of his
mannerisms by crying at him in the shower tent,
"Gentlemen only," or calling to him at bedtime,
"Tuck me in?" The clerk's so wrought up ("Careful,"
the boys in Demirgian's squad say, "careful, he'll hit
you with his purse")—so angry that not in a zillion
years will he see a bronze star and a "V" for valor
hung on any friend of Demirgian's. Instead, the clerk,
who every morning, afternoon, and evening has dis-*

.... he left unsaid, he has signed it with his commander's scratchy signature, and he has wished it Godspeed on the winding road to higher headquarters. One month later the very handsome medal is his.

". . . Through his untiring efforts and professional ability, he constantly obtained outstanding results. The energetic application of his extensive knowledge has materially contributed to the efforts of the United States Mission to the Republic of Vietnam to assist that country in ridding itself of the communist threat to its freedom. His initiative, zeal, sound judgment, and devotion to duty have been in the highest traditions of. . . ."

Eleven-thirty. Midnight almost, and Demirgian still hadn't met a communist, a passerby to fire his bright golden bullet at or throw his grenade at and kill.

One click—one kilometer—from the area where the passing hours went by Demirgian's ambush party like a trickle of lukewarm water was Demirgian's company camp, a tight little triangular area of huts and holes in the starlight, a Kipling place. Just outside of these earthworks, the Coke stand, as soldiers called it, was deserted, of course, it was closed until dawn, but that afternoon as Vietnamese small businessmen stood at its shaky wooden tables to give soldiers beer and Coke, to busily pop bottle tops off with rusty openers, to grow a garden of bottle tops in their fatherland's soil, to overcharge, and to shout at their weary customers not to walk off with the empties—that afternoon at the Coke stand something very strange had happened. Sitting drinking a bottle of Vietnam's formaldehyde beer, a soldier in this company had sought to fill up the empty interstices of time by saying one of those two or three formula phrases whose endless iteration passes for conversation at the Coke stand, "Hey mamasan, VC come tonight?" A catechism, but that afternoon instead of her cackling laugh and inveterate answer, "VC no come tonight," the Vietnamese in her clothes of black wrinkled rayon had looked at the soldier scaredly and quietly said, "Yes."

Now, it must be understood that the loud little people who worked at the Coke stand, dirt in each crease of their bodies, teeth the color of cockroaches, the words in their skinny mouths a caterwaul of ugly *ow* sounds—that the Vietnamese were a people whom the Coke stand customers had very little respect for, Demirgian, in fact, had even wanted to murder them, at times. Once in his early days in Vietnam he had bought himself an orange pop, he had given the lady a fifty-piaster bill, the Vietnamese had pushed it into the dirty seam of her dress—Demirgian had said quite politely, "Change?" At that, the lady had started to shriek—to *shriek* in the half-hysterical *ow*'s of a dog when there's somebody on its tail, to shriek at Demirgian and the echoing acres that fifty piasters—half an American dollar—was a fair market price for a bottle of pop in Asia. It was seven o'clock in the morning, and Demirgian's ears were used to the unbroken silence of the ambush party that he had been lying in all that night to guarantee the right of this shrieking lady to engage in private enterprise. It rankled Demirgian to think that he

...~~~~ ~~~~~ angry enough to do this.
But he didn't—Demirgian was very tired, anyhow he
had left his rifle up against a palm tree ten or fifteen
meters away. He didn't murder the Vietnamese
lady.

Still, the customers at the Coke stand had precious
little use for the counterwomen there. It was
"Mamasan, give me Coke" and "Mamasan, you
VC?" and *"Di di!"* to the little children who practically crawled in their ears as they crowded around
for C-ration chewing gum or candy—"Go!" the only
word of Vietnamese that all American soldiers knew
by heart, just as the Coke-stand crowd and prosti-
tutes were the only citizens of Vietnam that any soldier knew on sight. Among the Americans it was an
article of faith that the longer the Vietnamese war
would last the happier the Vietnamese people would
be—war to them meant money, even the salmon-size
cans of C-rations that the soldiers gave to those
screaming children went to their mamasans the
same afternoon to sell on the Vietnamese black market ("Or give to the VC," Demirgian used to say).
Our allies, our comrades in arms—the boys in Demirgian's company didn't think of the Vietnamese as
that, enemies, in fact, is closer to what these soldiers
thought of the native people, in fact their word for
things sold at those rickety tables was "VC beer" or
"VC orange pop" or "VC Coke." And these were the
boys whose predispositions the mamasan's answer of

that strange afternoon had fallen upon: "Hey mama-san, VC come tonight?" "Yes."

No one at the Coke stand believed her. Someone had wanted to notify the Captain—no! a sergeant had argued, the Captain he hears about this, he gets nervous in the service, he calls a hundred percent alert and who of us here's going to get to sleep? So forget it! And this is why at eleven-thirty most of those in the dark company camp or Demirgian's little ambush party were sound asleep in their camouflage-colored blankets unaware that a full battalion of communists lay in the blackness in range of Demirgian's peaceful rifle. Any minute now, they would attack.

WHAT DID YOU DO IN THE WAR, DADDY-O? *Five seconds. Four seconds. Three seconds. Two seconds. One—*

A soldier in a lightly starched tan uniform is keeping an eye on a wall clock that is somewhere about as large as the harvest moon. For a minute now, he hasn't taken a puff on the cigarette that he grips in his motionless fingers, he hasn't spoken a word since he whispered, "Out—out," to a boy so innocent of the circumstances that he had just walked into the quiet electronic-looking room.

At zero the soldier's impatient finger taps on a button of green—go! A circle of gray steel rotates, acetate issues, it interrupts the quanta discriminately, electrons are correspondingly let loose, a shower of electromagnetism falls on Vietnam as thoroughly as the monsoon rain—not a grain of rice escapes it. On earth, at a thousand electrical receptors all is reconstituted into the luminous images of Batman and Robin. Holy von Clausewitz, it's the Armed Forces Television Network! Zow!

... the ground, *ta-ta-ta-ta*, machine guns, the *bang* and *bang* of distant rifles, Demirgian also could look at things—the yellow sky, yellow because of the falling flares, the yellow sky shrinking in and around like a tired tent, a tracer bullet's long arc of red, another. Demirgian sat through this *son et lumière* with no great intellectual curiosity, things in the night were no great surprise to Demirgian, he was thoroughly used to them in Vietnam, war is war. He didn't guess that his company camp was under attack by two or three running hundreds of real actual communists, one kilometer away.

This startling news, the sergeant who prayed in Spanish had just heard in soft crackling sentences on the warm rubbery "telephone" receiver of an Army field radio. To this smart soldier, his elbows in the stony soil, the receiver tight to his attentive ear—to this experienced leader of the ambush party the news translated itself into an order of the highest urgency—*nobody should fire!* "Look," he said in a whisper to his radio operator, a PFC, a shadowy mass at his side—"look, we been cut off. Charlie got the trails going to the company block now. Is no way that we can penetrate back to the company. We—"

"How about the company?" the radio operator asked him. He knew if the company fell the squad wouldn't have a prayer.

"They are still fighting like good ones. We going to have to stay sweat 'im out. So it will be no fire," the sergeant said—*"it will be no fire unless they attack us.*" One little rifle sound, one little ray of red-orange light, one little grenade explosion and it was clear to this squad leader that the many companies of Charlies in the dark middle distance, advancing, retreating, giving themselves their pep talks, go give 'em hell, comrade, the Charlies would know of their whereabouts, not a boy on this lonely detachment would be left alive. A matter of their life and death, and to impress everyone on this perilous ambush party with the strategy of *don't shoot,* the sergeant said to the radio operator that he would crawl on the dark ground ten, twenty, thirty meters to the invisible figures on their left, the radio operator was to crawl to their right—to Demirgian.

Thus at about midnight, the radio operator, a good-looking guy, a Negro with light skin, thick hair, was doing what was without precedent in his many quiet nights on ambush parties: he was moving. His chest in the cold earth, his knees and elbows going like the claws of crabs, the pebbles going by beneath his stomach, the *o-o-o-o-o*'s going over, the *crump*'s, as the radio operator crawled by the strange shapes of night he was asking himself, *what am I doing this for?* He was on a madman's errand, that was a fact. To tell Demirgian that he must abandon his heart's desire, arrest his every instinct, keep his itchy finger from the trigger of his rifle or the cotter pin of his little grenade no matter how many black presences passed in the night—this was an act of saintly restraint that a whole heavenly choir of angels couldn't easily urge on that hellcat, easier tell a rattlesnake to ignore a rat! Moreover, the order of *don't shoot at the enemy* couldn't even be offered for Demirgian's consideration until the Negro radio operator had come within earshot—and rifle shot, it couldn't be delivered to Demirgian until the quietly crawling soldier was a target to Demirgian's wide-awake eyes. *What's with Demirgian?* often the radio

pop at the Coke stand with? Demirgian was a real
spitfire, the radio operator knew—was it something
psychological, perhaps? Had the Irish kids who
called him a camel chaser now become sublimated
into Asian revolutionaries? Or did Demirgian suffer
inferiority feelings, a year in Vietnam in the wilds
and woolies and he still hadn't proved himself, he
didn't have a scalp to show although other boys did?
Or simply, did Demirgian want to get written about
in *Newsweek,* that's all? *His forearms were being
slashed by thorns, his fatigues were.* . . . Many times
the radio operator had asked himself the question:
what is Demirgian bugged by, never, though, had he
guessed at Demirgian's secret, he hadn't come close.
He had satisfied himself by thinking, *well—Demirgian's an Armenian, that is the answer.* He had seen
a show on television about the Gurkhas once, the
Gurkhas all swinging a sword and taking a slice at a
living breathing ox, a splash, a bucket of blood, an ox
head lay on the ground like a rotten melon—a fierce
race of people, obviously enough, and Demirgian had
Armenian ancestors, Demirgian's family traced itself to the Gurkha part of the world. *That is the
answer,* the radio operator had told himself—mistakenly.

He had crawled over the stones to five or ten yards
from Demirgian's position—close enough, and he
whispered a word in the darkness that he knew
would identify him to Demirgian as a bona fide

friend from the Army, no communist. The radio operator whispered, "Demirgian!"

He heard Demirgian answer, "Yeah?"

The radio operator whispered to him, "Don't fire no matter what," and turning a hundred and eighty degrees he quickly crawled back to the dark patch of earth he had started at, where he opened a cold can of C-rations. His favorite kind of C-rats was turkey loaf—it was everybody's, it disappeared from the boxes quickly and tonight he was making do with boneless chicken, at least it wasn't the Spam ham and lima beans: *ugh!* a little wet pillar of salt, a cattle lick. With his GI opener in between his thumb and index finger he went to work experiencedly on that chicken can, the opener going as silently and as surely as a knitting needle, the tracer bullets making a *slap—slap*—as they passed above him. The skies were as yellow as Mars's, in the distances yellow smoke rose, at every horizon the heaven and earth seemed to have jarred apart, the yellow bowl of heaven rocked on the dark brown earth and—*boom! boom!* the universe, it seemed, was against the rocks, it was breaking up.

The radio operator heard a man whisper, *"What are you doing?"*

He answered truthfully, "Sergeant, when I'm hungry I eat." He buried his empty chicken can in cold earth, and with his little knitting-needle tool he quietly split the circumferences of a pound cake and fruit cocktail, thinking, *all I need now is vanilla ice cream—mm,* exactly as mother used to make it! The noises continued, *o-o-o-o-o! crump!* For his midnight crawl the radio operator was to get other desserts than C-rats, the Army commendation medal with a "V" for valor ("His actions are in keeping with the finest traditions of the military service . . .").

Demirgian. As for Demirgian, the infantryman *terrible* had given a good minute's thought to the

women or children but it wasn't anything new to Demirgian's ears and eyes. Old soldier Demirgian let himself forget it. At twelve o'clock his long boring hours of guard duty ended, and rolling over in the damp earth he whispered to a sleeping sergeant, "Hey. Wake up," for staying awake was that man's responsibility now. Then as the skies issued sounds like a house of a thousand shutters in a September storm, Demirgian rolled on his shoulder blades and closing his tired eyes he fell asleep.

Meanwhile, back at the camp. . . . *Back at Demirgian's triangular camp the Captain is shouting things to his company with his shotgun in one hand and flip-flops on his feet—Vietnamese rubber shower shoes, he hadn't time to dress, a lieutenant is thinking worriedly what's with the mortars? Why don't the company mortars fire? The first sergeant is lying wounded, the enemy is fifty—forty—thirty yards away and coming closer. Running to where the mortars are, crying why aren't they being fired, told we are waiting for data, sir, we need to be given our azimuth data, our elevation data, our increment data, our— hearing this, the lieutenant cries one of the inspired cries of the twentieth century, let history record that the lieutenant cries, "The hell with data!" And seizing the mortar tube in his sweating hands he says to start dropping the mortar rounds in—and crump!*

crump! he levels them on the charging communists. From out of the west come the hoofbeats of water buffalo, the lone lieutenant cries again, the lieutenant says, "The buffalo are coming! And they—" the lieutenant means the enemy soldiers, "they are right behind them," the mortars turn to the water buffalo, the buffalo are turning back! The communists are being buffalo-bumped! But now there is one more mortar round left in that beleaguered camp—no more. The mortarmen kiss it, caress it, slip it into their mortar tube, it exits, the mortar round falls in the midst of America's enemies with a bump, it doesn't go crump! All is quiet on the mortar front! Boo to American industry!

The communists still keep coming—damn. The camp is frightfully shy of rifle soldiers, some are in Army hospitals, irregular holes in their arms or legs, malaria, gonorrhea, some are on pacification work and Demirgian is fast asleep, the artillery officer is a playboy in Tokyo on a rest and recreation leave, a terror-stricken lieutenant is still in his little cotton tent, his shoes shined, his belt buckle bright with metal polish. Outside of the company camp the barbed wire is absent—orders, we've got to show the Vietnamese we aren't a bunch of scaredies, damn! On one whole side of the triangle not a rifle is functioning, double damn—the bullets are stuck inside of them and of the machine guns, too! Boo to Connecticut! Nuts to the Nutmeg State! The communists are coming over the earthen walls now! Are we downhearted? YES! As soon as they've taken the company camp the little abandoned ambush party is next!

And meanwhile Demirgian sleeps through it all (When the bough breaks, the cradle will fall).

position, to his stomach. The silhouette of a hip, a shoulder going over, an arm—anything, the sergeant had told himself, would be just enough to notify whoever was making all those shooting sounds in the night, the *o-o-o-o-o*'s and the *crump*'s, the *ta-ta-ta-ta-ta*'s like a cold motor, the rifle shots, of his presence on this lonely square yard of earth, and he stayed on his back during his whole tour of guard duty. Inconspicuousness—the secret of one's survival.

He could look at the stars. Years ago, he had become aware that as stars go across the Carolina night they aren't like wild ducks, the stars aren't shoving themselves one ahead of the other or slipping behind, the star patterns that he could see in the Carolina sky didn't change for hours—for years, and when he had come to Vietnam he was pleased to see that these special relationships one to the other held for that alien land, as well. He looked at these familiar faces now in his motionless hours of standing guard—of his lying on guard, the prism, the rocking chair, the cup and the saucer, these are what the sergeant called his precious constellations. Low in that friendly sky was the "V" shape of Taurus the bull, to the sergeant this was part of a spaceship, the nose cone. Orion at this season lay on its side horizontally, its belt became a bandleader's hat to the sergeant's nostalgic eyes, its sword was a celluloid visor—the sergeant remembered the golden braid in its broad figure eights, the sergeant could even see it! The silver whistle, the shiny scepter, a downbeat hard as a hand on a wooden table, *be kind to your web-footed friends!* The sergeant had been a bandleader once—at a high school for Negroes he had played on the drums, the clarinet, the bass and baritone tubas, he hadn't cared to play the trombone, it didn't ever get to solo, still he liked the guitar the best, really and truly. Tonight while he lay on his back on sentry duty he sang to himself sentimentally, *He took a hundred pounds of clay and He said, Hey listen! I'm goin' to fix this world today because I know what's missin'!* A pretty song—it reminded him of his wife in Scotland Neck, North Carolina.

Being in Vietnam made the sergeant want to sing, a melody held the minutes together in a way that simply twiddling his fingers didn't, time was as thin as skimmed milk if the sergeant didn't fill it with remembered songs. Demirgian he didn't understand at *all*, Demirgian for whom every second patch of elephant grass was enough to make the senses quicken, the eyes become as lively as a chirping bird's, the life forces start to flow, Demirgian who looked for a destructible enemy in every second cranny of every paddy even as the sergeant tried to keep acedia away by singing to himself, *can't get no . . . satisfaction.* "Demirgian. Now take it easy," often the sergeant had to preach patience to Demirgian when the disappointed soldier shot at the pigeons and people's chickens after yet another day of not shooting communists. Demirgian's mysterious vendetta wasn't— well, it wasn't a vendetta even, the sergeant knew. Not a boy in Demirgian's whole platoon had been killed or wounded by *communists* since the first days of Demirgian's tour of duty. Accidents do happen and Demirgian had many friends who weren't alive any longer, still he couldn't fault the communists for something as American in its origins as "I didn't know it was loaded" ways of behavior, this the ser-

Buddhist monk, it wasn't the fault of the Bolsheviki—any of those. Seven whole boys (a lieutenant, even) had shot themselves in this or that anatomical organ in the course of one particularly ridiculous week, the fault was in themselves and Demirgian wasn't out for revenge, obviously enough—his ferocity wasn't due to this. *Must be, Demirgian had a brother killed,* the sergeant had told himself: untrue. Demirgian the fire-eating soldier, a mystery to that sergeant lying beside him.

"*I love you,*" the sergeant was thinking now.

"*No, no!*"

"*Yes, I love you. You are more to me than anything in the whole world,*" the line was Lord Darlington's in *Lady Windermere's Fan,* by Oscar Wilde. Who would have guessed as that sergeant lay in his dirty combat clothes as the *o-o-o-o-o*'s and the *crumps*'s reverberated and as time itself seemed to condense from the night air to settle around him as damp as a heavy dew—that the Negro sergeant had once played the Darlington part in his segregated high school's big auditorium, an ascot around his neck, in its center a pearl stickpin, the hints of his acting teacher firm in his senses: say *rawther* instead of *rather,* cup in the right hand and saucer in the left. The line of Wilde's he remembered most was "Excuse me, you fellows. I have to write a few letters," the sergeant had given it many earnest reprises, the teacher had been in the wings with a script, whenever the sergeant's half-open mouth had failed to entice one of

199

Darlington's speeches to fill it with apropos sounds he had simply said, "Excuse me, you fellows. . . ."

Uh-oh. A squad of little communists was quietly coming along the trail—the sergeant didn't see it since he hadn't eyes on top of his head, and Demirgian the wistful communist-killer was fast asleep.

A tragic happening. *Bang! Bang! At the company camp the enemy has broken through, a corner of that black triangle is communist-held—a bunker, inside it a couple of Coke bottles, bottle caps, the colorful crumbs of fruitcake, pound cake in a C-ration can, a can that is empty, lids, a couple of comic books, ten or a dozen Playmates, mosquito repellent, cigarettes, the empty brass of Connecticut's bullets—that, and some communist soldiers too. American boys are throwing the last of the hand grenades with a Batman abandon, one soldier not even pausing to pull out the cotter pin. But there come the reinforcements—hurrah! The resupply of ammunition, the high-explosive rounds, the phosphorus, the bullets made in Connecticut by sweet old ladies in steel shoes—the ammo is coming along the trail in a steel tank and bang! it suddenly explodes, the tank, the mighty ammunition too. The communists on their ambush party are luckier on this awful night than Demirgian on his.*

From out of the smoking top of the tank wreck a tank soldier crawls. A lieutenant, his clothes are in terrible shreds, one of his legs isn't there, he hasn't one of his arms, instead of his genital organs there is a bleeding hole, the phosphorus has gone through his eyeballs, they are like glowing charcoals—they are like orange "exit" bulbs. From now until dawn he will crawl on the scorching steel, then he will be flown to Washington to recuperate.

story. Three hours out of Saigon's ridiculous airport,
ten thousand planes, the planes in the treetops almost, the planes sitting one on the other like the
gray arrays at automobile graveyards, the noise, the
inconsiderateness, the Vietnamese people—three
hours after this and Demirgian had been dining in
quiet luxury in the land of white elephants, the setting immaculate, a candle, a low teak table reposing
like a tamed lion on a purple rug, a picture window,
a curtain made of tissue-paper flowers as delicate as
moths, and seen through it a garden, the wind was in
the palm trees, a star. Everything in that restaurant
in Bangkok shone, and music as soft as water running over a bed of pebbles quietly came to Demirgian
from—where? it had seemed to Demirgian that molecule on molecule of air just tapped onto one another
like little tinkling cat bells, Bangkok! It had been a
real revelation, he had never guessed that the Orient offered things to the senses other than the sight
of running noses, the smell of sewage in streets. In
this first delightful hour in Bangkok, girls in purple
silk hostess gowns had come to Demirgian smiling
adoringly, crawling to him on their reverential
knees with a pitcher of water or wine, apologizing to
Demirgian for entering upon his serenity uninvited,
forgive me for saying so except . . . the flowers, the
petals are meant to delight the palate as well as the
wondering eyes, the petals are a finely carved chestnut. Crawling to Demirgian, one of these orchid girls
had given him a silver silk bag of Bangkok's per-

fume, the girl herself whispering thank you—thank you! Never before in Asia had Demirgian heard the words thank you, even the loud little children that he had left chewing gum in the grabby little hands of had never said *cam on* in Vietnamese, they had simply shoved out their other hand. Bangkok had just enchanted him, it didn't smell of deteriorating fish, it had traffic lights, lines in the center of its wide streets, it seemed that the people of Bangkok *cared*, the barbers—even the barbers had worn white doctors' robes and had shaved off the fluff on Demirgian's eyelids and inside his ear canals, sending a small squirt of water in afterward, what a wonderful country! Demirgian said to some friends, "If they had a war here, I'd reenlist if I could go to Thailand, wouldn't you?"

His friends had said yes. Demirgian had taken this leave (the Army called it a rest and recreation leave, and every boy in Vietnam whether he kills an enemy soldier or doesn't has a week of it in his year's tour of duty)—Demirgian had come to Bangkok with two good friends, the first was Demirgian's most immediate sergeant, a Botticelli angel boy, a sergeant with a sweet almost watery smile, eyes of calamine blue, the other was Demirgian's friendly lieutenant, the leader of his platoon. A real source of humor this—if Demirgian asked him, "Do you have a match," the lieutenant would say something like, "I don't light a cigarette for a private, *private*," the lieutenant lighting it anyhow, the three of them laughing, friends in Bermudas and sports shirts. After the wine, the chestnut carved like a frangipani flower, the Thai girls with fingers like cattails doing a delicate dance, the music of gentle stringed instruments—after the candlelit dinner the three boys had gone to a nightclub, the sergeant had fallen in love: Keri, the young girl's name. The rest of that wonderful week the three were a foursome as Keri showed

so her laughter wouldn't go beyond the bounds of her people's sense of etiquette.

On the seventh day they had visited the zoo, the monkeys swinging there like indian clubs, a black arm, a leg, a tail of each spider monkey twisted around the steel trapezes, the graceful, surprisingly, giraffes, the elephants like an Egyptian relief, a row of them standing all looking left, a rope on their enormous legs to orient them in that direction, the elephants rocking side to side as slowly as heavy punkahs on hot afternoons, the trunks of these elephants swinging, the ears slowly moving like old shredded regimental flags—it seemed that these monumental elephants had been standing there through all Asian history, swaying side to side. Above the center elephant was a high golden roof—a temple roof, its millions of little sequins the color of old mustard shone in the Bangkok sun, and Keri had said almost reverentially, "This is the King's elephant."

Demirgian had asked her cheerfully, "Which is the Queen's elephant?" and Keri had suddenly turned away looking hurt. "Aw," Demirgian said in embarrassment. "Doesn't the Queen have an elephant?" and Keri got rigidly silent.

"You shouldn't make fun of their king and queen," the soft-spoken sergeant told him.

"I'm not making fun," Demirgian answered honestly. "Which is the King's giraffe?" But every lighthearted thing that Demirgian thought of saying to

Keri so she would smile again, Keri just got angrier at, her lips got tighter together, the sergeant got quite apprehensive. "I wish I were a king so I could have an elephant," Demirgian tried—it didn't work, to a Thai there's little to say of their benevolent king and queen except perhaps hosanna. "Hey," Demirgian said in some despair. "Let's do the dodger cars," and he ran from those difficult elephants to a nearby kind of Playland park—he was already in a blue miniature car, he was driving it every which way, he was—*crash*—he was crashing it into the native people by the time the others, surprised, had come walking up. "Everyone let's do *this,*" Demirgian drove to them shouting.

The lieutenant wasn't too terribly sure. "I don't think the Thais are as barbaric as we are, Demirgian," the lieutenant said, the Thais in the other dodger cars were driving them, in fact, as gingerly as A&P shopping carts, the Thais were smiling to one another, tipping their hats, in effect, and acting as though they had only learner's permits till Demirgian charged at them, Demirgian who—*zzzzz*—was suddenly off again in a cloud of concrete dust, the terror of the Thai five hundred, the wheels rising, the tires crying, the side of his steel sports car was *crash! crash!* was crashing on everyone else's, the metal getting dented, the shower of sparks, the Thais in their battered chariots all laughing happily and Keri, at last, laughing, too, Keri now sitting on a bench because of her laughing so hard, the sergeant laughing, the lieutenant laughing and crying, "Go gettem, cat! Go gettem," Demirgian laughing triumphantly, the Grand Prix of Bangkok his.

In the evening they ate at the river, the sunset lay on the temple tops and slivers of orange sunset fell in the silver river and drifted by like goldfish. Keri said to the real catfish, "Here, baby. Here," giving the fish little bits of bread to nibble on. That night Keri

landed when the three soldiers met a Guamanian
friend from their own platoon, the lieutenant naturally asking him, "What's new?" Well, in Vietnam it
had been another of those stupid weeks, the Guamanian said—Demirgian's best friend, the medal-less
communist-killer, had been lying on ambush when
he was taken for Charlie and accidentally shot in the
head by a squad sergeant and, well, the platoon sergeant had been killed one morning at reveille by
American artillery, idiotically one of our howitzers
had been aimed at his sleeping bag, so it's hi-dee-hee
in the field artillery and, of course, the first sergeant,
he had been telling guys to police up this, police up
that, exactly as some clumsy son-of-a-dumbbell
stepped on a detonator and *bang!* as *police up* died on
the first sergeant's lips the first sergeant himself
had died and also, a company next to theirs, uninten-
tionally it had been bombed by American airplanes,
twenty or thirty soldiers were in the hospital for napalm burns, another twenty or thirty boys died and—
anyhow, it had been a bad week, the Guamanian
stated, you couldn't really deny it. Demirgian went
to buy a hot dog saying to Keri's sergeant, "Vietnam! The cesspool of the universe!"

"The cesspool of the universe," the sergeant re-
peated—he was shaking uncontrollably now. He was
still acting strange the next afternoon ("He looked
like he was underwater," a boy remembered)—the
next afternoon when he got to his quarters: the company camp, a dark canvas tent, a long row of cots, a

205

couple of Vietnamese laundry boys on one of them, sitting, looking at dirty photographs of ways of making love, and saying things in English like "Fucky-fucky," laughing, letting their wide red palates show. Putting one of Connecticut's bright bullets in his rifle chamber, *click! clack!* the sergeant said, "I'm going to do some hunting."

"I hope you'll do your hunting out yonder," the soldier who owned the photographs said to him uneasily.

"I can do my hunting right here," the sergeant replied. Once he had killed the Vietnamese laundry boys he was taken away in handcuffs and was court-martialed. At present, the sergeant's serving a life sentence at Leavenworth, the Negro who looked at constellations and sang *can't get no . . . satisfaction* taking his place as Demirgian's sergeant.

A question from the court. *"Were these dirty pictures of American women?"*

"They were just some old dirty pictures you buy around." The witness is the soldier who owned them.

"Were there oriental women in them? Or were they caucasian—white—women?"

"Oriental."

"Pictures of oriental women?"

"Yes sir."

"Were there dirty pictures of oriental men or caucasian men?"

"Oriental men. They had masks on, some of them."

"The dirty pictures consisted of both oriental men and oriental women?"

"Yes sir."

"There were no white women in those pictures?"

"No sir."

"But if a man had on a mask, now would you know?"

"Well, he didn't look American, sir."

"What didn't look American?"

"The man. There was something about him that was oriental."

"I repeat my question. What didn't look American?"

"The whole bunch! The pictures! They weren't American!"

A PART OF THE DEFENSE'S SUMMATION. "He goes to his tent to get ready to go to the field—to pick up his equipment. After entering he sees the two Vietnamese for whom he has no love or trust, sitting on the bunks, talking, laughing, and enjoying themselves. He explains to himself, why should he fight in their country on their behalf and risk his life for these people while they perform menial tasks at the base camp in the relative safety of the base camp. As he gathers his equipment perhaps he thinks about this. Maybe he becomes angry. . . ."

A PART OF THE PROSECUTION'S SUMMATION. ". . . Well, okay, he disliked the Vietnamese, fine. That's up to an individual. If he wants to hate the Vietnamese, fine! But putting his hatred in action by killing is not quite correct."

"Huh?" Demirgian said.

The other boys in the ambush party had waked up Demirgian an hour before dawn and related to him what great alarms and excursions there were while God had His guardian angels over him—the company camp had been attacked, a corner taken, a tank carrying ammo had been blown to kingdom come, a second tank had gotten into the triangle, *tarantara*, the tide of war turning, communists withdrawing, company enduring, hurrah! Not a boy in Demirgian's sturdy army had been killed by those two or three or four hundred communists (one had been killed accidentally by an American, nothing more) —a very great victory for America. By the wet yellow light of the flares, Demirgian could now glimpse some of the forty or fifty communist dead, the easy victims of American artillery and of six-barreled machine guns on American planes, fat fire-breathing planes that the soldiers had given the sobriquet of Puff the Magic Dragon *(. . . lived by the sea,* the Negro sergeant had sung to himself at one o'clock in the morning, the magic dragon's rain of red tracer bullets lighting the night with a pillar of fire—*lived by the sea, and frolicked in the autumn mist in a land called Honah Lee).*

Good soldiers all, nobody in the ambush party had shot at that communist squad when it innocently went by, the silver starlight above it, behind it, the final score had been nothing to nothing, the ambush party the communists. Demirgian got to his heavy feet, the bullet still in Demirgian's dew-dappled rifle like a disappointed suitor, the hand grenades still on Demirgian's belt, mud in the crack of their cotter pins, corrosion, dew. *Damn, but I would have fired at them,* Demirgian angrily said to

well deserved, now he was kicking one of those soldiers every bit as hard and shouting at their unlistening ears, "Wake up, you silly bastard—you sorry bastard—you stupid bastard! Wake up!"

"Hey, Demirgian," somebody said to him, laughing. "They're already dead."

"Wake up, you goddam bastard," Demirgian said to one dead communist, kicking.

"Demirgian," the Negro radio operator said to him softly. "Don't do that."

"What do you mean don't do that?" Demirgian asked.

"Don't do that," the Negro radio operator said. He didn't like to see brutality, the radio operator—once he had been in a street gang, he was twelve years old, at a gas station he had gotten into a fight with the white-colored kids. It had been simply sticks till a two-tone automobile had driven by, a Negro, he was twenty, perhaps, had gotten out of that great automobile, he had squatted on the chest of one white boy, he had raised up a concrete block and—*down,* the boy's white face had broken apart like a bag of blood, the fight had stopped immediately. Running, everyone running, the Negro radio operator running, a fruit cart toppling over, the grapes rolling after him like little bloodshot eyeballs, running, falling, the dirty red blood on his elbows, after the Negro child reached home he had prayed all night, "Oh Lord! Don't let him die!" Since then the Negro radio operator had disliked brutality—yet, he

thought, how could there be brutality if the communists felt no pain, if the sufferers were already dead,
if the bodies lay every random way as though they
had fallen from airplanes, Demirgian kicking, calling them dirty bastards, mud of his boots spattering
on the yellow faces, the skin of the faces shivering
like mud under raindrops—uncomfortably, the radio
operator walking away as Demirgian still kicked at
them calling, "Wake up!" But none of the communist soldiers woke up.

One of the communist soldiers woke up! He looked
at Demirgian slowly through one of his yellow eyes,
an eye like a twist of lemon rind, an oily eye! He
lifted one of his bloody arms! A living breathing communist, a boy of about eighteen, a Vietnamese in
crinkled black, Demirgian brought down his foot on
his face and *crunch,* Demirgian felt his little nose go
like a macaroon, he said to the communist, "Bastard—well, was it worth it," kicking him in his
eyeballs. "Stupid bastard—what did it get you,"
kicking him on his Adam's apple. "Goddamn bastard. . . ."

D emirgian's secret. *Demirgian hates the Vietnamese people—well, so does every soldier, but
Demirgian hates and hates! The goddamn bastards!
Goddamn people! Come to help their miserable country and what? Anyone get any thanks? No, dead or
alive—crippled, I could be blind, a basket case and
they wouldn't care, not if they had my damn piasters
first! Money is all they care, the crooked bastards!
Give me—give me—that's the extent of it, give 'em a
stick of soap, though, do you suppose they'd use it, the
filthy people? No—they'd sell it, the filthy bastards!
Nya nya nasal language, they sound like they've got
their tongue up their nose, the ugly bastards! Faces*

A really and truly detestable race of people. Demir-
gian's year of duty among the Vietnamese had taught
him to loathe them, the earth and Demirgian would
be better rid of them, Vietnamese go to your damnable
ancestors, die! Demirgian wants to kill communists
because they're the only natives the Army's regula-
tions allow him to kill.

" . . . Dumb bastard, stupid bastard, goddam bastard, thought you were better than us Americans, didn't you? Ignorant bastard," Demirgian said
and he kicked at that black bag of bones until it had
given a consummation to Demirgian's tour of duty
and a high success to Demirgian's quest by quietly
becoming dead. Congratulations, Demirgian's foot!
For it hadn't been by Connecticut's fancily manufac-
tured bullets that he had achieved his heart's desire,
Demirgian had become a communist-killer by force
of foot alone—Agnes's dustpan hadn't been necessary, David's leather mallet neither, America could
have saved itself money, each of those bullets cost it
ten cents.

"Sorry about that," Demirgian said to the lifeless
body, and he continued toward camp by the dawn's
early light, a Russian watch in his pants pocket—a
souvenir.

Like a great headache going, a pressure on the

ears relieved, the black of night receded into the skies and a pink sunrise came to that company camp, the tents became green, not gray, the brass of Connecticut's bullets lay on the earth like little bright buttercups. A couple of tired soldiers went to police the bodies up, another was at the washbasin brushing his teeth, spitting the pink water into the Vietnamese mud, a toe slowly turning it under and stirring the liquidy pink and brown, washing, drying himself, his olive-colored towel wet with the morning dew, another was having coffee from a gray aluminum cup, the gritty metallic taste of aluminum oxide on his tongue, nails in a carpenter's mouth. It was morning and each soldier said to himself *so-and-so-many days,* each was a day nearer to getting out of that abominated country. Six o'clock at the Coke stand it was business as usual, the Vietnamese women with their betel-black teeth, the raggedy tan piaster notes, the sticky yellow dribbles of paint on the soda bottles so soldiers wouldn't want to take the empties away, the price of four times the wholesale price, the heat, the children on those tired soldiers saying *give me—give me—*and saying dirty words if they didn't get given, a Vietnamese shouting at the exhausted soldiers, *"Ong da ban chet. . . ,"* the mortar rounds had wounded one of his water buffalo, he wanted compensation. "Well," Demirgian said to another soldier, "I finally killed me a gook," and Demirgian smiled satisfiedly, Demirgian's soul was at peace, Demirgian, a little later, started back to the country in whose interests he had been posted to Asia, to his green gabled home in Massachusetts, to the sign in the living room *welcome home* in red, white, and blue! Safe and sound, Demirgian came marching home again! Let's give him a hearty welcome then! Hurrah! Hurrah!

admiration to A—who...
of Amarillo, Texas, *"Out—out"* ☆ Master Sergeant Raymond H. Admire of Ravenna, Ohio, *"Don't fall in them"* ☆ Staff Sergeant Bernardo Agosto-Ramos of Fort Dix, New Jersey, who filed it one month before throwing it away ☆ Staff Sergeant Doroteo Q. Aguigui of Agat, Guam, who is the Guamanian ☆ Staff Sergeant William O. Allen of Chieflands, Florida ☆ Captain Harold T. Amaker of Falls Church, Virginia ☆ Private Douglas H. Arrington of Newark, New Jersey ☆ Colonel Claude E. Bailey, Junior, of Chattanooga, Tennessee, who cautiously routed it to the General ☆ Staff Sergeant Noah I. Bailey of Columbus, Georgia, *"Keep alert!"* ☆ Second Lieutenant Victor J. Bedard of Westmoreland Depot, New Hampshire, *"The men couldn't grasp the pistol"* ☆ Specialist 4 Elie J. Benoit of Fitchburg, Massachusetts, *"Hey Doc!"* ☆ Major Homer G. Benton of North Hollywood, California, *"Courage"* ☆ Private Vaughan A. Bigalow of Medford, Oregon ☆ Private First Class Charles H. Blanchet of St. Louis, Missouri, who worked at M's finance office ☆ Second Lieutenant Arthur M. Bliss, Junior, of San Antonio, Texas, *"He's selfish, he's unpatriotic"* ☆ Warrant Officer 4 David J. Blumen of Pacific Grove, California, who is Fu Manchu ☆ Private First Class Jimmy E. Boan of Chesterfield, South Carolina, who was killed on Thursday ☆ Sergeant First Class Felipe Bonilla-Viera of Aguadilla, Puerto Rico, who was killed on Thursday ☆ Specialist 4 Leonard E.

215

Brock of Hyden, Kentucky, *"Damn, we've got to sew those stripes on"* ☆ Colonel William D. Brodbeck of Junction City, Kansas, Sullivan served him roast beef ☆ First Lieutenant James F. Brown of Huntsville, Alabama, *"Fool's mate!"* ☆ Staff Sergeant Lonnie Brown, Junior, of Killeen, Texas, *"What are you doing?"* ☆ Captain Terry W. Brown of New Orleans, Louisiana, *"I repeat my question. What didn't look American?"* ☆ Specialist 4 Allen G. Bruederle of Cedarburg, Wisconsin, *"Last name! First name! Middle initial!"* ☆ Specialist 5 Harmon C. Burd of Fayetteville, North Carolina, who was killed on Wednesday ☆ Major Solomon A. Card, Junior, of Leonardsville, New York, *"I rise on a point of personal privilege"* ☆ Specialist 4 Donald A. Carlisle of Concord, California, Demirgian told him, *"I finally killed me a gook"* ☆ Captain Raymond A. Carucci of Mount Vernon, New York, *"Man! This puts hair on your chest!"* *"He's been nominated, he can't decline!"* ☆ Second Lieutenant Thomas E. Chorba of Dickson City, Pennsylvania ☆ Private Samuel J. Cobaris of Orlando, Florida, who forgot that it snowed in Europe ☆ Private Joe C. Cobb of Piedmont, Alabama, *"When you're old they'll throw you away"* ☆ Sergeant Lawrence E. Collins of Clinton, Tennessee, *"About . . . face!"* ☆ Private Alan B. Collinson of Biloxi, Mississippi, Sullivan told him *"Wake up!"* ☆ Sergeant Patrick Condron of Lakewood, New Jersey, the bullet went through his helmet, *"I'm going to do some hunting"* ☆ Private Ernest L. Contrera of Brooklyn, New York, *"This is like Coney island,"* *"Coward!"* ☆ Private Harold W. Cooper of Milpitas, California, *"The lieutenant doesn't want you to"* ☆ Private First Class Merton E. Dawson, Junior, of New York, New York, who watched through a periscope ☆ Private Al De Carlo of Schenectady, New York, who said it wasn't 84 but 94 ☆ Private Varoujan Demirgian of Newton, Mas-

T. Doherty of Fort Dix, New Jersey ☆ Private George B. Dubitsky of Shamokin, Pennsylvania, who looked like a Chinese pagoda ☆ First Sergeant Oliver D. Dumas of Atlanta, Georgia, *"Police up"* ☆ Colonel Paul J. Durbin of Washington, D.C., *"Were these dirty pictures of American women?"* ☆ Major George L. Egbert of Ludington, Michigan, Sajo gave him a swivel chair ☆ Brigadier General William E. Ekman of St. Louis, Missouri ☆ First Lieutenant Benny R. Ellis of Springfield, Missouri, *"Beer coming up"* ☆ First Sergeant Robert E. Enlow of Accident, Maryland, *"You've got to wear a steel pot!"* ☆ Private Arliss L. Faust of Cincinnati, Ohio, *"I'd talk to him"* ☆ Lieutenant Colonel Paul M. Fisher of Clyde, Nebraska, *"Insure that positive identification be made"* ☆ Private Billy J. Fite of Dallas, Texas, whose rifle caught on some brambles, *"No person owns one thing"* ☆ Staff Sergeant Robert Foley of Elmont, New York ☆ Private Edward Franklin of St. Albans, New York, who wore mittens ☆ Private First Class Robert T. Gammie of Ventura, California, who shooed away the flies ☆ Private First Class Benjamin G. Gardiner of Waltham, Massachusetts, who scored 147 ☆ Private William R. Gardner of Philadelphia, Pennsylvania, *"I got winners,"* *"What's the matter with Chaska?"* ☆ Private First Class George W. Garrison, Junior, of Owensboro, Kentucky, who quietly snored ☆ Private Louis A. Giarrusso of Johnston, Rhode Island, who went ahead of the line of fire ☆ Sergeant Shelby Gore of

Pacoima, California ☆ Staff Sergeant Norman L. Guessford of Smyrna, Delaware, *"We did it up in thirty-six hours"* ☆ Sergeant J. Gutierrez-Santiago of Fort Dix, New Jersey, who said Orientals don't go to Vietnam, *"Okay! He is wounded—right?"* ☆ Private First Class Ronald Halovanic of Pittsburgh, Pennsylvania, *"Of course they'll be VC sympathizers"* ☆ Private Thomas P. Hanlon of Warren, Ohio, *"Twenty dollars!"* ☆ Private Lorin R. Hardman of Murray, Utah, Hofelder was in front of his rifle ☆ Private David E. Hazelwood of Sumter, South Carolina, *"He was born in a cave"* ☆ Staff Sergeant Donald L. Heaston of Columbus, Georgia, the howitzers had been aimed at his sleeping bag ☆ Sergeant Cephas L. Hembry of Washington, District of Columbia, *"What have you did?"* ☆ Private First Class Donald J. Hibbs of Philadelphia, Pennsylvania, *"There's nothing to be done"* ☆ Sergeant Dallas E. Hickman of Parkersburg, West Virginia ☆ Sergeant Roy Hickman of Nashville, Arkansas, *"We've got to stitch them"* ☆ Private First Class Fred S. Higdon of Tampa, Florida ☆ Staff Sergeant Thomas E. Hinton of Tampa, Florida, the flute player ☆ Private Joseph J. Hofelder of Philadelphia, Pennsylvania ☆ Private Rodney W. Houle of Burlington, Vermont, *"I'm me and he's he"* ☆ Specialist 4 John C. Howard of Cincinnati, Ohio, *"We're sorry"* ☆ Sergeant First Class Jesse A. Isaac of Neshoba, Mississippi, *"Americans—surrender!"* ☆ Sergeant John Y. Jackson of Philadelphia, Pennsylvania, who sucked a toothpick ☆ Private William J. Jackson of Paterson, New Jersey, who fired a one-gun salute ☆ Master Sergeant Robert Jarosz of Joliet, Illinois, who put the Bible in footlockers ☆ Specialist 4 Gerald E. Jett of Rockville, Indiana, *"Well maybe I'm stupid," "Let's go, gentlemen"* ☆ Specialist 4 Billy L. Johns of St. Cloud, Florida, whose name was spelled wrong in *Newsweek* ☆ Specialist 4 Fred D. Johnson nior, of Binghamton, New York, who played tic-tac-toe ☆ Second Lieutenant David Kinkead of Clearfield, Pennsylvania, *"These people don't want us here anyhow"* ☆ Staff Sergeant José Lamar-Guerra of Puerto Nuevo, Puerto Rico, the baritone player ☆ Major General J. C. Lambert of Washington, Arkansas, the footlocker general ☆ Private Theodore C. Landers of Somerville, New Jersey, *"How can I go home this weekend?" "We're all cowards"* ☆ Private First Class James E. Larkin of Flint, Michigan, *"If they're not a VC now they'll be one after"* ☆ First Lieutenant Stephen F. Ledger of Newton Falls, Ohio, *"VD City"* ☆ Staff Sergeant John R. Lehman of Chicago, Illinois, *"You're not winning friends among Vietnamese farmers"* ☆ First Lieutenant Frederic H. Leigh of Dayton, Ohio, *"Texas on this side! California on this side!"* ☆ Major Stewart K. Lewis of Easton, Pennsylvania, *"Kill the umpire kind of thing"* ☆ Sergeant David J. Lippert of Washington, District of Columbia, *"Rock steady!"* ☆ Lieutenant Colonel Gordon J. Lippman of Council Grove, Kansas, who was killed by a Vietnamese villager ☆ Captain Clyde R. Locke of New York, New York, *"Environmental dangers"* ☆ Specialist 4 Claude G. Lumbeck of Richmond Heights, Missouri, *"I have a headache"* ☆ Private James M. McCarthy of Mattituck, New York, *"How can I get married now?"* ☆ Private Charles T. McCorkle of Bradshaw, Maryland, the Major told him to shave ☆ Private First Class Wayne McFarland of Millville, New Jersey, who is Swizzlestick ☆ Private First Class James Ripple McMichael of Youngstown, Ohio, *"Hurry up! Faster!"* ☆ Private First Class John J. Maher of Baltimore, Maryland, *"Sergeant, he's not my congressman"* ☆ Staff Sergeant Nathaniel Mallory of Fort Dix, New Jersey ☆ Private Maurice J. Marier of Verdun, Quebec, Prochaska told him, *"A major hasn't the time"* ☆ Private Bernard Mason of New York, New York ☆ First Sergeant Robert E. Mason of Worcester, Massachusetts, who made terrible threats to Williams ☆ Private Clarence R. Matheson, Junior, of Garland, Texas, *"Were you born in a barn?"* ☆ Sergeant First Class Alec J. Matisco of Roanoke, Virginia, *"Watch and see!"* who gave M a chalk talk on horseshoe ambushes ☆ Platoon Sergeant Oswald Medina of San Antonio, Texas, *"Sir, there's a little girl"* ☆ Second Lieutenant Mark J. Meirowitz of Pittsfield, Massachusetts, the bullet struck his Star of David ☆ Sergeant Emilio P. Milett of Fort Dix, New Jersey ☆ Captain Edward S. Molnar of Cleveland, Ohio, *"If he wants to hate the Vietnamese, fine"* ☆ Private First Class Hector R. Morales of The Bronx, New York, *"I don't know, you know the Army"* ☆ First Lieutenant Juan A. Morales of Rio Piedra, Puerto Rico, the lieutenant of *"The lieutenant doesn't want you to"* ☆ Major Richard L. Morgan of Monte Vista, Colorado, *"Bob? You're in a hospital"* ☆ Private Billy W. Morton of Wichita Falls, Texas ☆ Captain Douglas J. Nelson of Concord, North Carolina, *"Many were the generous tears"* ☆ Private William M. Newman of Salem, Florida, *"Now it's so cold"* ☆ First Sergeant Julius M. Panikowski of Cheektowaga, New York, who was lying wounded ☆ Specialist 4 John G. Patten of Shadyside, Maryland, *"He looked like he was underwater"* ☆ Captain Philip E. Pelino of Chicago, Illinois, *"Sir, you're out of order!"* ☆ Platoon Sergeant Walter J. Penchikowski of Dorchester, Massachu-

Specialist 4 David L. Toland of Lincoln, Nebraska, *"Room in a harem"* ✩ Captain Ronald H. Tuman of Charleroi, Pennsylvania, *"He only earns his freedom and existence"* ✩ Private Kenneth A. Varney of Tonawanda, New York, *"Trust and obey God's word"* ✩ Sergeant First Class Donald Van Walker of El Reno, Oklahoma, who blew up the maple sugar ✩ First Lieutenant Emmett J. Ward of Gretna, Virginia, *"I guess he is really hauling one!"* *"Punji pits,"* *"I think we should burn the rice harvest too"* ✩ Major Michael L. Wardinski of Chicago, Illinois, who is Iron Mike ✩ Private Joseph K. Watson, Junior, of Lewiston, Pennsylvania, whose rifle looked like a little umbrella ✩ Private Melvin Williams of Plant City, Florida ✩ Private First Class Clyde W. Withee of Skowhegan, Maine, who was mortally wounded on Wednesday ✩ Second Lieutenant Helen Ann Yazzie of Santa Fe, New Mexico, who pulled up the bedsheet ✩ Private Bob H. Yoshioka of Los Angeles, California ✩ and everyone else in M and in the Army.